Computer Science Workbench

Editor: Tosiyasu L. Kunii

Computer Science Workbench

N. Magnenat Thalmann, D. Thalmann: Image Synthesis. Theory and Practice. XV, 400 pp., 223 figs., including 80 in color. 1987

B.A. Barsky: Computer Graphics and Geometric Modeling Using Beta-splines. IX, 156 pp., 85 figs., including 31 in color. 1987

H. Kitagawa, T.L. Kunii: The Unnormalized Relational Data Model. For Office Form Processor Design. XIII, 164 pp., 78 figs. 1989

N. Magnenat Thalmann, D. Thalmann: Computer Animation. Theory and Practice. Second Revised Edition. XIII, 245 pp., 156 figs., including 73 in color. 1990

N. Magnenat Thalmann, D. Thalmann: Synthetic Actors in Computer-Generated 3D Films. X, 129 pp., 133 figs., including 83 in color. 1990

K. Fujimura: Motion Planning in Dynamic Environments. XIII, 178 pp., 85 figs. 1991

M. Suk, S.M. Bhandarkar: Three-Dimensional Object Recognition from Range Images. XXII, 308 pp., 107 figs. 1992

H. Ishikawa: Object-Oriented Database System. Design and Implementation for Advanced Applications. XVIII, 166 pp., 38 figs. 1993

Hiroshi Ishikawa

Object-Oriented Database System

Design and Implementation for
Advanced Applications

With 38 Figures

Springer-Verlag Tokyo Berlin Heidelberg New York
London Paris Hong Kong Barcelona Budapest

DR. HIROSHI ISHIKAWA
Fujitsu Laboratories Ltd
1015 Kamikodanaka, Nakahara-ku
Kawasaki
Kanagawa, 211 Japan

Series Editor:
PROF. DR. TOSIYASU L. KUNII
President and Professor
The University of Aizu
Tsuruga, Ikki-machi
Aizu-Wakamatsu
Fukushima, 965 Japan

ISBN-13: 978-4-431-68310-0   e-ISBN-13: 978-4-431-68308-7
DOI: 10.1007/ 978-4-431-68308-7

Printed on acid-free paper

© Springer-Verlag Tokyo 1993
Softcover reprint of the hardcover 1st edition 1993

Series Preface

Computer Science Workbench is a monograph series which will provide you with an in-depth working knowledge of current developments in computer technology. Every volume in this series will deal with a topic of importance in computer science and elaborate on how you yourself can build systems related to the main theme. You will be able to develop a variety of systems, including computer software tools, computer graphics, computer animation, database management systems, and computer-aided design and manufacturing systems. Computer Science Workbench represents an important new contribution in the field of practical computer technology.

Tosiyasu L. Kunii

Preface

The goal of this book is to give concrete answers to questions such as what object-oriented databases are, why they are needed, how they are implemented, and how they are applied, by describing a research prototype object-oriented database system called Jasmine. That is, this book is aimed at creating a consistent view to object-oriented databases. The contents of this book are directly based on the results of the Jasmine project conducted at Fujitsu Laboratories, Ltd. The book is a polished version of my doctoral dissertation, which includes research papers which I have authored and published.

We started the Jasmine project around 1985 with the aim of developing a next-generation database system for data- and knowledge-intensive applications such as Computer-Aided Design (CAD), hypermedia, and Artificial Intelligence (AI). The main goals of Jasmine are:

    (1) Natural modeling of complex data such as component hierarchies, multimedia data, and knowledge

    (2) Natural modeling of behaviors associated with complex data

    (3) Flexible manipulation of large amounts of complex data

    (4) Reasonable performance of storing and accessing large amounts of complex data

To give a better understanding of Jasmine, I briefly explain research projects prior to and relevant to Jasmine in which I was involved at Fujitsu Laboratories, Ltd. We had research projects on relational databases and on natural language interfaces to relational databases. Such intelligent interfaces require semantically rich data models to understand and represent the meanings of natural language queries. To this end, we developed an object-oriented data model on top of relational databases. And we devised an object-oriented programming language in harmony with object-oriented data models for efficient and flexible programming, in particular, representing behavioral knowledge. As a result, we confirmed the basic validity of our object-oriented approach to modeling complex data and behavioral knowledge.

However, our approach at that time imposed the burden of describing mappings between objects and relations on the users (sophisticated users). Then we wished to develop a next-generation database system for advanced complex applications which could efficiently store large-scale objects used by object-oriented programming into databases, and which could retrieve and manipulate them without the need of the user mapping. This initiated the Jasmine project. The concept of an object-oriented database has been a natural consequence from the beginning.

Our object-oriented database system Jasmine has rather sound technological foundations. Jasmine draws upon previous researches on databases, programming languages, and artificial intelligence. As for the data modeling, Jasmine borrows concepts such as classification (classes), generalization (class hierarchies), aggregation (complex objects), derivation from semantic data modeling in databases. Jasmine borrows concepts such as demons (triggers) and annotations (integrity constraints) from frames in artificial intelligence. Jasmine borrows concepts such as methods and polymorphism from object-oriented programming languages. Jasmine integrates such concepts into a unified framework. In contrast, there are many object-oriented databases which have data models based only on object concepts of object-oriented programming.

As for the data manipulation language, Jasmine has aimed to integrate a query language facility (set-oriented access) and a programming facility (individual access) from the beginning. The query language extends the functionality of SQL by incorporating object-oriented concepts such as complex objects, class hierarchies, and methods into SQL-like languages. In contrast, many other object-oriented databases add on query languages afterwards, since they mainly attempt to extend object-oriented programming.

As for the implementation, Jasmine takes advantage of a large volume of relational technology such as storage structures, access methods, query optimization, and transaction management. Of course, Jasmine extends such techniques for object-oriented functionality. In reality, Jasmine efficiently stores objects in nested relations and directly manipulates objects on page buffers. Many object-oriented databases make little use of relational techniques.

In other words, the Jasmine project attempts to build a practical semantic database system enhanced with dynamic facilities on top of extended relational database and object-oriented programming language techniques. Like this, Jasmine has been constructed from a wide range of technological perspectives. I believe that it doesn't impair the generality of this book if I take Jasmine as an object-oriented database and describe its functionality and implementation.

Of course, Jasmine is an attempt to overcome the limitations of relational databases and object-oriented programming languages alone. In particular, the limitations become evident when they are being solely applied to large-scale complex applications rather than business applications. In other words, the characteristics of Jasmine become salient when Jasmine is being applied to such advanced applications. Therefore, we devote many pages in this book to nontrivial applications such as CAD, hypermedia, and AI. This book does not intend to explain a wide variety of object-oriented databases. Instead, it aims to give a consistent understanding of object-oriented databases by describing the functionality, implementation, and applications of Jasmine. To understand other object-oriented databases, one has only to understand their differences from Jasmine. I believe a deep understanding of a single object-oriented database system is a better way to grasp the essence of object-oriented databases in general.

This book consists of eight chapters. Chapter 1 describes the characteristics of advanced applications to explain why object-oriented databases are needed. Chapter 8 makes concluding remarks. The remaining chapters are divided into two parts. Chapters 2, 3, and 4 describe the functionality and implementation of object-oriented databases to define what object-oriented databases are. Chapters 5, 6, and 7 describe concrete applications of object-oriented databases to present how object-oriented databases are applied.

Chapter 1, INTRODUCTION, discusses the salient features of advanced applications such as CAD, hypermedia, and AI. This chapter describes the need for a next-generation database system to enable users to construct such advanced applications.

Chapter 2, DATA MODEL, describes the basic concepts of object-oriented databases and the semantics of the data model. The basic concepts include attributes, methods, classes, instances, object identifiers, complex objects, class hierarchies, constraints, and demons. The formal definition of the model semantics is also described.

Chapter 3, DATABASE PROGRAMMING LANGUAGE, explains the data manipulation language of object-oriented databases. This chapter describes set-oriented access (query) and individual access (programming) of objects. The query language is extended to incorporate object-oriented concepts, such as object identifiers, complex objects, methods, and class hierarchies. The chapter also introduces concepts such as derivation methods and set variables to explain how query and programming facilities are integrated. The formal definition of the query semantics is also described.

Chapter 4, IMPLEMENTATION, describes how object-oriented databases are implemented. The system architecture of Jasmine consists of data management and object management subsystems. The data management subsystem provides nested relations and their operators. The extended relational operators can take manipulation and predicate functions as their parameters which can directly access tuples on page buffers. The object management takes advantage of the data management to efficiently store and access objects. Object-oriented query optimization and object buffering are also discussed in detail.

Chapter 5, ARTIFICIAL INTELLIGENCE APPLICATIONS, describes an object-oriented approach to AI applications. This chapter focuses on an object-oriented model and programming language devised for a natural language interface to relational databases, which is a precursor of Jasmine. This chapter also discusses the basic validity of integrating object-oriented data modeling and programming.

Chapter 6, HYPERMEDIA APPLICATIONS, discusses the limitations of current hypermedia systems when they are being applied to large-scale complex applications. This chapter then describes solutions to the issues by using an object-oriented database approach.

Chapter 7, ENGINEERING APPLICATIONS, discusses the issues of mechanical engineering. These include design data management, intelligent CAD support, and engineering information management. This chapter describes an object-oriented database approach to them.

Chapter 8, CONCLUSION, makes a brief survey of research prototypes and commercial database systems and compares Jasmine with them. This chapter concludes the book by describing the future research issues of object-oriented databases.

I assume that the readers of this book have a certain level of basic knowledge about relational databases and programming languages. The first group of readers are graduates and undergraduates in advanced database courses. This book gives them the fundamental concepts, functionality, and implementation of object-oriented databases. This book provides designers and implementors of object-oriented databases with sufficient knowledge about the design and implementation of object-oriented database systems. This book also aims to help those who will be applying object-oriented databases to their problem domains. Those who want to know about the functionality and implementation should read Chapters 1, 2, 3, 4, and 8. The rest is optional. Those who want to know about applications should read Chapters 1, 2, and 3 and choose among Chapters 5, 6, and 7. The rest is optional.

Jasmine is one of the earliest projects on object-oriented databases. To my knowledge, Orion at MCC started around the same time. In fact, different research groups have started object-oriented database projects independently. This is an example of concurrent scientific discoveries and is similar to parallel evolutions in biology. I believe that, in that sense, the concept of an object-oriented database itself is a natural consequence.

When the Jasmine project started, we sometimes found it rather difficult to make others understand what object-oriented databases are. Nowadays, however, there are many commercial systems and research prototypes and more and more people are becoming interested in object-oriented databases. We feel that the situation has improved surprisingly. I am fortunate because I have observed the emergence and evolution of a new research field from the very beginning. I hope that readers will see the past, present, and future of object-oriented databases through reading this book.

Hiroshi Ishikawa
Kawasaki, Japan

Acknowledgements

I would first like to thank my principal dissertation advisor, Professor Tosiyasu L. Kunii, of The University of Tokyo, for his professional suggestions, encouragement, and help. I am also very grateful to the other members of my dissertation committee, Professor Akinori Yonezawa of The University of Tokyo and Associate Professor Mamoru Maekawa of The University of Tokyo (currently Professor of The University of Electro-Communications), Professor Yahiko Kambayashi of Kyoto University, and Associate Professor Yasushi Kiyoki of University of Tsukuba for their helpful suggestions. I thank Miss Yuka Hirahara of Springer-Verlag for her editorial help and patience.

Many people at Fujitsu Laboratories, Ltd. have been very supportive. I thank Mr. Mikio Otsuki, Mr. Shigeru Sato, Mr. Jun'ichi Tanahashi, Dr. Takao Uehara, Mr. Hiromu Hayashi, Dr. Nobuaki Kawato, Dr. Akifumi Makinouchi (currently Professor of Kyushu University), Mr. Yoshio Izumida, Mr. Etsuo Ono, Dr. Tatsuya Hayashi, Mr. Masayoshi Tezuka, Mr. Yasuo Yamane, Mr. Fumio Suzuki, Mr. Masaaki Aoshima, Ms. Mika Miyagishima, Mr. Toshiaki Yoshino, Dr. Tadashi Hoshiai, Mr. Kazuhiro Ohishi, Dr. Fumihiro Maruyama, Dr. Haruo Yokota, and Dr. Lilian Harada.

Finally, I thank my wife Tazuko Ishikawa, my father Tomoyuki Ishikawa, my mother Shizue Ishikawa, my brother Akira Ishikawa, my son Takashi Ishikawa, and my daughter Hitomi Ishikawa for their encouragement, support, and patience.

Contents

Chapter 1
INTRODUCTION

1.1 Motivation

New database applications such as computer-aided design (CAD), artificial intelligence (AI), and hypermedia [HALA88], have emerged. Some of the special requirements which a conventional relational database system cannot satisfy are as follows:

(1) CAD systems [MITT86a] find optimal solutions to design problems efficiently by using domain-specific knowledge. AI-based natural language interfaces use a *world model* [ISHI87] or *generic knowledge* about domains for understanding user queries. In contrast, data which conventional relational database systems manage can be considered as *factual knowledge*. The applications must be able to maintain both generic and factual knowledge.

(2) CAD and hypermedia applications require *complex objects* [HASK82] such as component hierarchies and structured texts. AI systems use complex objects to represent deep domain knowledge such as a world model rather than shallow knowledge such as production rules. Although relational database systems can simulate complex objects by joining relations, they impose unnecessary burdens on the user in modeling and performance. The applications must be able to represent complex objects directly and implement them efficiently.

(3) CAD systems use a graphical representation of layout plans. Hypermedia systems store and retrieve images and text. AI applications use graphics to present information to the user and to interact with the user. The applications must be able to integratedly store and manipulate *multimedia data* (images, graphics, and texts) in addition to numbers and strings which relational database systems are good at handling. The application programs must allow the user to *directly manipulate* multimedia data [SHNE83].

(4) CAD systems use dynamic characteristics of components as *behavioral knowledge* first recognized in AI, which relational database systems cannot handle.

Hypermedia applications retrieve data by content-based searching and manipulate the data in addition to simple browsing. The application systems must be able to manage such behavioral knowledge explicitly. In addition, the application systems must be able to flexibly develop *active databases* [MORG83] such as maintaining consistency by using triggers. Ultimately, the whole knowledge-based application systems must be programmed in a unified, general-purpose programming language.

(5) CAD and hypermedia systems require large amounts of knowledge such as whole components and images. All of this knowledge cannot reside in main memory at the same time. The application systems must be able to efficiently store and access such voluminous knowledge and run at a reasonable speed. To this end, the application programs must integrate and extend the *compiler* technique of a programming language and the *query optimization* technique of a relational database system.

(6) The application systems are not fixed but are evolutionary. Hypermedia systems may require the incorporation of new media such as audio and geometric data. The user must be able to flexibly define new types and associated operations and new access methods. The inclusion of new types, operators, and access methods must be done with as little modification as possible. Conventional database systems cannot handle this.

Systems supporting the development of these advanced application systems are called a *next-generation DBMS*. The sophisticated user (application programmer) builds an application system by using a next-generation DBMS. The inexperienced user uses the completed application system. "Users" in the context of this thesis means sophisticated users. The implementation of a next-generation DBMS requires extension and integration of the technology for databases, programming languages, and artificial intelligence.

An object-oriented approach in programming languages [GOLD83][STEF86] is also promising for use in a next-generation DBMS for the following reasons. Objects can support complex objects directly and represent behavioral knowledge as methods [STEF86]. Since multimedia must be specified both structurally and behaviorally, it can be naturally modeled by objects. An integrated interface can be given to media methods which perform the same function but have different implementations depending on the types of media. This feature of objects is called *polymorphism* [STEF86].

However, the object-oriented approaches currently being used have several drawbacks. From the viewpoint of extensibility, the object model semantics are not clear enough for the user to understand and construct a model easily. From the viewpoint of application programming, the object-oriented programming language must be extended because it operates on objects only individually and lacks associative access of objects needed by most applications. In other words, current object-oriented programming languages are not set-oriented while relational databases are. Current languages cannot handle a large number of objects efficiently. They cannot support *object persistency* [BLOO87].

1.2 Overview

In this thesis we describe how we solved these problems and how we designed and implemented an object-oriented DBMS called *Jasmine* [ISHI88][ISHI93a] as a next-generation DBMS. We can summarize our research contributions focusing on the object model, object manipulation language, and implementation of Jasmine as follows. First, our object model is based on the *functional data model* [SHIP81] and well-established set-theory. Attributes or functions composing objects can represent both structural and behavioral knowledge. Objects are uniquely identified by system-generated object identifiers. Objects containing object identifiers as attribute values can represent complex objects logically. *Nested relations* [ROTH88] representing complex objects can cluster complex objects physically. The system provides a sufficient number of system-defined objects to make possible a wide variety of applications. The built-in objects also contain a self-description of the model semantics and multimedia objects. The introduction of *facets* or *demons* [MINS75] leads to a flexible description of integrity constraints for an attribute and of triggers for an active database. A generalization hierarchy supports attribute inheritance. Any class object in a generalization hierarchy can have instance objects so that the user can express incomplete knowledge about the domain. We can formally describe the semantics of our object model.

Our object manipulation language has the following features as a database programming language. The language supports associative access of objects and direct access of complex objects without explicit joins. The language enables methods to be invoked in any part of associative query so that the user can retrieve objects with a complex search and manipulate retrieved objects compactly. The language integrates individual access of objects for a general-purpose programming language and set-oriented access of objects for a database by supporting method invocation in a query, method definition by a query, and set object variables. The basic operations of multimedia are supported to ease development of multimedia applications. Generic knowledge is operated on in the same way as factual knowledge. A variety of demons can be invoked with object access to implement triggers. Incomplete knowledge specified by a nonleaf class in a generalization hierarchy can be flexibly accessed. Uniform treatment of system-defined and user-defined methods allows for user customization of the language without modifying the language processor. We can formally describe the semantics of the query through query translation by object operators.

To efficiently support the object model and object manipulation language, we developed a general-purpose extended relational database system called *XRDB* [YAMA89] and provided the object model and operations on top of XRDB. XRDB supports nested relations and associated operators and a variety of access methods such as *dynamic hashing* [LARS80] and B-trees to support efficient storage and access of objects in secondary memory. To efficiently implement procedural knowledge, XRDB allows the user to define predicate and manipulation functions which can be compiled to operate on tuples in the buffer directly. User access to objects is compiled to do early binding and avoid run-time overhead. During compilation, query optimization including complex object access, incomplete knowledge access, and method invocation is done. The layered architecture provides more flexibility than a monolithic DBMS. The run-time support accelerates object access by using a dedicated mechanism such as an internal hash table, or object buffering.

This thesis is organized as follows. Chapter 2 describes the semantics of our object model as the data model. Chapter 3 presents the object manipulation language based on the object model semantics. Chapter 4 describes the implementation of the object model and language. Chapter 5, 6, and 7 discuss object-oriented database approaches to artificial intelligence, hypermedia, and engineering applications, respectively. Chapter 8 compares our system with other related work and gives concluding remarks.

Chapter 2
DATA MODEL

This chapter describes an object-oriented data model of Jasmine [ISHI93a]. The object model of an object-oriented database for advanced applications has the features different from those of the relational model. We can summarize the features of the Jasmine object model as follows.

Objects are categorized into instances and classes. Instances denote individual data and classes denote types and operations applicable to instances of the class. Objects have system-generated object identifiers by which they are system-wide uniquely identified. Object identifiers contain class identifiers, so the inspection of an object identifier of an object can determine the class to which the object belongs without looking up of the content of the object. An object has more than one attributes. An object has both a single value and a set of values as its attribute value. An object can have object identifiers as well as atomic values such as numbers and strings as its attribute value. Complex objects can be logically modeled by the attribute containing object identifiers (aggregation). Unlike other systems, Jasmine also enables the physical clustering of complex objects by nested relations. A class is a collection of attribute definitions. A class defines the type and operations of the instances by enumerated attributes called properties and procedural attributes called methods. In a word, properties and methods can model objects structurally and behaviorally. Unlike other systems, Jasmine allows the user to specify both system-defined integrity constraints such as mandatory, multiple, and to specify arbitrary user-defined integrity constraints as demons attached to attributes. A class contains instances which belong to the class (classification). A partial order relationship holds between similar classes (generalization). Through the relationship, classes are organized into a class hierarchy, or a superclass-subclass hierarchy. A subclass inherits properties and methods from its superclass. A subclass is set-included by its superclass. The user can define arbitrary data types by combining existing ones through classification, aggregation, generalization, and behavioral modeling, whose semantics can be formally defined.

2.1 Object Semantics

We describe semantics of objects which are an integration of a functional data model and *frames* [MINS75] in AI. Objects are a collection of attributes, which represent structural and behavioral knowledge of a domain directly. Attributes are categorized into *enumerated attributes* and *procedural attributes*. Enumerated attributes are used to represent structural knowledge such as Name and Doctor. Procedural attributes are used to represent behavioral knowledge (programs) such as make-medical-certificate. Although an enumerated attribute and a procedural attribute correspond to *slot* and *method* [STEF86], they can be uniformly treated in the object manipulation language as described in Chapter 3. Objects are categorized into *instances* denoting individual knowledge, or factual knowledge, and *classes* defining attributes applicable to similar instances, or generic knowledge. In this section we describe object semantics focusing on *aggregation* [SMIT77]. *Classification* [SCHR84] and *generalization* [SMIT77] are described in Section 2.2.

We define attributes based on functions in a functional data model. An attribute is a mapping from a set of objects to a set of objects. In general, the attribute takes a set of objects as input and gives a set of objects as output. In particular, if the attribute returns a set of one element (*singleton set*), it is viewed as returning an object rather than a set. An attribute which always returns a singleton set is called a *singleton-valued attribute*. An attribute which possibly returns a set of objects, not a singleton, is called a *multiple-valued attribute*. A multiple-valued attribute taking a set of objects, not a singleton, such as union and unique, is called a *set function*. A singleton-valued attribute taking a set of objects, not a singleton, such as count and sum, is called an *aggregate function*. The set in our context is a *bag* [SHIP81], a set which allows duplicates of objects. The terms function and attribute are interchangeably used in this thesis.

Objects are identified by an *object identifier* (OID) [KHOS86]. An OID is generated by the system and represented by the system-defined attribute Oid which the user can reference. An object with an OID is called a *reference object*. In contrast, string and number objects have only values, no OID. Such objects are called *immediate objects*. Immediate objects can only exist in an attribute, so they are not sharable. It is impossible to modify immediate objects directly. Immediate attributes, attributes whose values are immediate objects, are just changed from the binding of a value to another binding. Reference objects are instantiated independently and referenced by attributes. Reference attributes, attributes whose values are reference objects, must satisfy *referential integrity* [DATE81]. Equality of reference objects are based on OID and equality of immediate objects are based on values. In a word, reference objects are first-class objects and immediate objects are pseudo objects.

```
PATIENT
        Db              MEDICAL
        Super           PERSON
        Enumerated      DOCTOR          Doctor    mandatory
                        STRING          Category            default "outpatient"
                        INTEGER         Cardinality      common
                        FLOAT Temperature       multiple
                                constraint {(value > 34.0 && value <43.0)}
                        FLOAT Weight    mandatory constraint {(value > 0.0)}
                        FLOAT Height    constraint {(value > 0.0)}
                                                If-needed
                                                { int h;
                                                h = self.Weight;
                                                return h + 100.0;}
        Procedural      MEDICAL_CERTIFICATE     make-medical-certificate (date)
                        STRING date;
                        { MEDICAL_CERTIFICATE  mc;
                        int i;
                        mc = <MEDICAL_CERTIFICATE>.instantiate ();
                        mc.Patientname = self.Name;
                        mc.Doctorname = self.Doctor.Name;
                        mc.Diseasename = self.Disease.name;
                        mc.Date = date;
                        return mc;}
```

Figure 2.1. Example of class definition.

```
MedicalPatient007
        Sex                     "male"
        Age                     36
        Name                    "James Bond"
        Address         "Tokyo"
        Doctor          MedicalDoctor010
        Category                "inpatient"
        Temperature             36.5 37.3 38.1
        Weight          76.0
        Height          181.0
```

Figure 2.2. Example of an instance.

A class defines attributes applicable to its instances, like a type in a programming language. Attributes consist of *facets* [MINS75] which denote functional annotation of the attribute and differentiate our object model from other functional data models [SHIP81] [FISH87]. Consider the class PATIENT as an example (See Figure 2.1). The keyword *Enumerated* is followed by the definition of user-supplied enumerated attributes. The *name* facet such as Doctor denotes the name of an attribute. The *class* facet before the name facet denotes the function range class such as FLOAT of Height. The value of the attribute of an instance must be an instance of the range class (see Figure 2.2). The compiler uses this constraint to check types statically. The functional domain of the attribute is the class being defined, PATIENT. The *multiple* facet denotes that the attribute is a multiple-valued function such as Temperature. The *mandatory* facet denotes that the attribute allows no null value such as Doctor and Weight (total function). The null value in an attribute denotes that the attribute value is unknown. The user can specify internal representation of null values for each class. The mandatory attribute, an attribute which is specified mandatory facet, must be specified its value at instantiation. The *common* facet denotes that the attribute value is common to all the instances as the domain objects. The common attribute, an attribute which is specified common facet, is not necessarily a constant such as Cardinality. The *default* facet contains a default value referenced when the attribute value is not yet specified, such as Category of PATIENT.

The behavioral knowledge can also be attached to the enumerated attribute. The knowledge is represented by the demon facets and invoked by different triggers. The procedure in the *constraint* facet, the *constraint demon*, is invoked before a value is inserted to the attribute. The value is set to the attribute only if the procedure returns true. Constraint demons such as Temperature can allow the user to specify more complex and general constraints than *object participation* of IRIS [LYNG87]. The *if-added demon* is invoked after the value is inserted into the attribute. The *if-removed demon* is invoked after the value is deleted from the attribute. The *if-updated demon* is invoked after the value is modified. The *if-needed demon*, invoked if the referenced attribute has a null value, computes a value such as Height of PATIENT. It is, so to speak, a procedural default. The default can be simulated by the if-needed demon, but the default is more explicit. The user can combine these demons to flexibly implement active databases.

The keyword *Procedural* is followed by the definition of user-supplied procedural attributes. Procedural attributes such as make-medical-certificate also have facets. The class facet such as MEDICAL_CERTIFICATE denotes the range class of the procedural function. In particular, if the procedural attribute returns a null value, system-defined VOID is specified as the range class. The multiple facet denotes multiplicity of the function result. The procedural attribute can take additional parameters such as date, in addition to the domain object. This realizes multiple-argument functions. Demons such as *before* and *after demons* which can be attached to the procedural attributes are used to check the preconditions of the main function and to propagate the side effect of the function [ISHI90].

The attributes are supplied by the user or the system. The system-defined attributes are used for a variety of functions as follows. The user can choose among sequential, B-tree, and dynamic hash relations as the storage structure of objects by the attribute *Storagetype*. The user can create indexes on arbitrary attributes by the attribute *Index*. The size of the pages for object storage is specified by the attribute *Pagesize*. The size of the internal hash table used by the run-time support to manage objects in main memory is specified to control conflict resolution by the attribute *Aotsize*. Other system-defined attributes include *Super*, *Class*, *Db*, and *Comments*. The attribute Super, Class, and Db denote generalization, classification, and a database.

As described above, objects can have arbitrary objects as an attribute value. Complex objects in general terms can thus be directly represented. The user can freely define new data types and associated operations as objects. Notice that the attribute name has only to be unique in a class. Different classes may have attributes of the same name with the same purpose but with different implementations. At invocation, an appropriate implementation is chosen depending on class types. This mechanism is unambiguous, eliminating the need for the concept of *role* [SHIP81][LYNG87].

2.2 Classification and Generalization

In this section we describe object semantics associated with classification and generalization. A class and its hierarchy are interpreted set-theoretically.

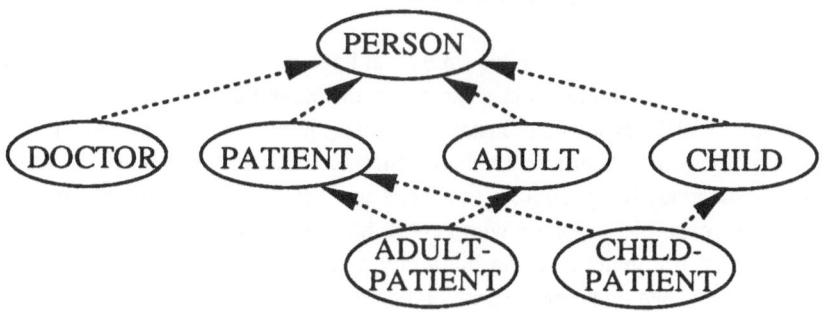

Figure 2.3 Example of a class lattice.

A class is not only a type defining characteristics common to its instances but is also viewed as a set of instances. For example, PERSON is a set of persons (See Figure 2.3). Our concept of class represents classification directly. This eliminates the need for extra concepts and simplifies the object manipulation language design. Unlike Jasmine, Smalltalk-80 [GOLD83] and its descendants such as GemStone [MAIE86] introduce a *collection* in addition to a class in our context.

An instance belongs to only one class intrinsically. The class is called *intrinsic class*; its instances are called *intrinsic instance*. If the user creates an instance from a class such as PATIENT by the system-defined procedural attribute instantiate, the instance is an intrinsic instance of the class PATIENT. The intrinsic class is denoted by the system-defined attribute Class. Consider an alternative which allows one instance to belong to more than one class. This alternative doesn't enable one class to provide full information of the whole instance. It is inappropriate for *model-based processing* [ISHI87] often appearing in AI which is mainly based on generic knowledge or classes. The alternative makes an object model less understandable and makes maintenance related to instance modification more complex.

The system-defined attribute Super supports generalization. The superclass, for example, PERSON, includes its subclasses, PATIENT, as a set. Instances of a subclass belong to the superclass virtually but not intrinsically. The interpretation of a class is the set union of the intrinsic instances of the class and the instances of its subclasses. A leaf class has only intrinsic instances. The characteristics which hold in the superclass hold in the subclass. Thus, the attributes of the superclass are inherited to the subclass, such as Age of PATIENT. The refinement of the attribute definition is possible by overriding facet descriptions. In particular, the range class of the attribute of the subclass is to be a subclass of the range class of the same attribute of the superclass. This is because incomplete knowledge access described below can retrieve the attribute values of the superclass and those of the subclass at the same time. An attribute can be newly defined in the subclass such as Doctor of PATIENT.

Any class in a generalization hierarchy can have its intrinsic instances. In particular, intrinsic instances of a nonleaf class can represent *incomplete knowledge* of the domain. For example, PERSON intrinsic instances directly denote a set of persons known to be neither a patient nor a doctor. Intrinsic instances can model the domain knowledge as it is. The instance may be specialized to a more specific class if new information is added in future. For example, a person who gets ill becomes a patient. An instance can move around classes in a generalization hierarchy as the database evolves. Unlike the IFO model [ABIT87], we make no distinction between generalization and specialization for simplicity.

A class is divided into disjoint subclasses. Those subclasses are collectively called a *partition*. Each subclass is called a *member* of the partition. For example, PERSON has a partition consisting of DOCTOR and PATIENT. A partition denotes a categorization based on one viewpoint. Different viewpoints generate different partitions. PERSON has another partition of ADULT and CHILD. Members of distinctive partitions may not be disjoint, such as PATIENT and ADULT. *Categorization conditions* can be explicitly specified to make the partition semantics clear such as "Age >= 18" of ADULT. Then the attribute Age is called a *categorization attribute*. The specification language of the categorization conditions is basically a subset of the knowledge base programming language described in Section 3. The conditions can be used by optimization described in Section 4.

Our semantics allows a class to have *multiple-superclasses.* They must be nondisjoint members of different partitions of a class. Since a subclass with multiple-superclasses is included by all of the superclasses and then by the intersection of them, disjoint superclasses would make the subclass empty. The attribute Super introduces a lattice [BANC86], not a strict hierarchy. The top is the system-defined OBJECT and the bottom is VOID. The greatest lower bound of subclasses is the most specialized common superclass such as PATIENT of ADULT-PATIENT and CHILD-PATIENT. The least upper bound is the most generalized common subclass such as ADULT-PATIENT of ADULT and PATIENT. The Super semantics also holds to multiple-superclasses. For example, ADULT-PATIENT inherits Doctor from PATIENT and Occupation from ADULT (*multiple-inheritance* [STEF87]).

Notice that we assume that if multiple-superclasses have attributes of the same name, they are usually defined only once in the common superclass. For example, Age of ADULT-PATIENT is defined in PERSON, but neither in ADULT nor in PATIENT. Of course, subclasses can redefine an attribute of the superclass by use of the subclass of the range class of the attribute. In such cases, conflict resolution is done by the system's depth-first search. However, if the user wants to give the same name to two attributes with different meanings, the user has to rename one of them explicitly. This assumption makes the model more understandable and the implementation simpler.

A class is an instance of the system-defined class CLASS. One purpose of this is to make our model as self-descriptive as possible. Another purpose is to be able to operate on classes and instances in a uniform fashion. Unlike TAXIS, we don't introduce *metaclasses* [MYLO80] which make the object model more complex because the management of the metaclass needs the extra concept of *metametaclass*. We describe CLASS in detail in Section 2.3.

2.3 System-Defined Classes

The system-defined classes constitute a kernel database of Jasmine (See Figure 2.4). The user can model the application domain by using these classes.

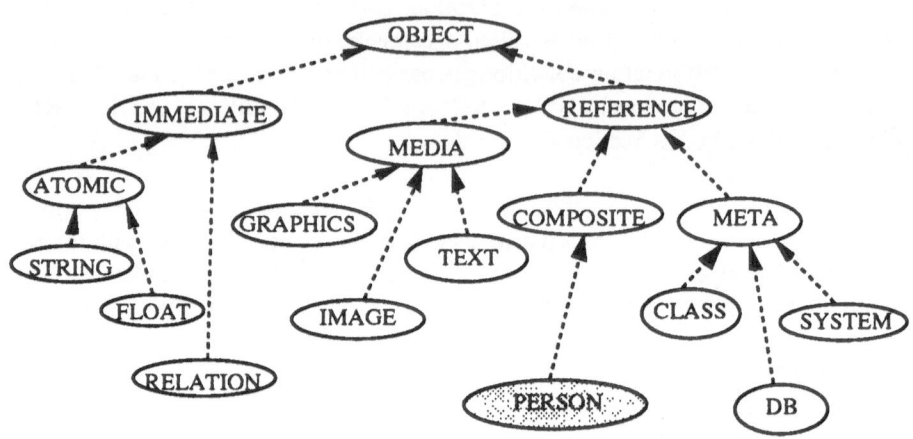

Figure 2.4. Part of system-defined classes.

The system-defined classes mirror the object model semantics. OBJECT is the root of an object lattice. OBJECT is divided into REFERENCE and IMMEDIATE denoting reference and immediate objects. IMMEDIATE objects are divided into ATOMIC and RELATION objects. ATOMIC objects include INTEGER, FLOAT, STRING, and VSTRING objects. RELATION objects can have both REFERENCE and IMMEDIATE objects as attribute values. RELATION objects realize nested relations [ROTH88] directly. Complex objects of ORION [BANE87] can be represented by using RELATION objects. The following constraint called *complex object integrity* holds in the whole-part relationship induced by the complex objects: The part objects don't exist before their whole objects do and the part objects are destroyed at the same time the whole objects are. A complex object in this sense is a collection of a whole object and its part objects as a unit. Nested relations realized by RELATION objects can cluster complex objects to satisfy complex object integrity both logically and physically.

System-defined classes have system-defined attributes which are inherited by the user-defined subclass. IMMEDIATE objects have procedural attributes. They include scan functions such as openscan, next, and closescan. In addition, ATOMIC objects have aggregate functions such as count, average, sum, max, and min. RELATION objects have count as an aggregate function.

REFERENCE has enumerated attributes such as Class and Oid. REFERENCE has procedural attributes such as put, replace, delete, and destroy in addition to scan functions. REFERENCE is divided into COMPOSITE, MEDIA, and META. The user usually defines domain objects as subclasses of COMPOSITE. MEDIA has subclasses IMAGE, GRAPHICS, and TEXT. They have polymorphic procedural attributes such as input, output, change-size, and move, which have different implementations from one media to another, but have the same interface. The user can operate on multimedia in a uniform interface.

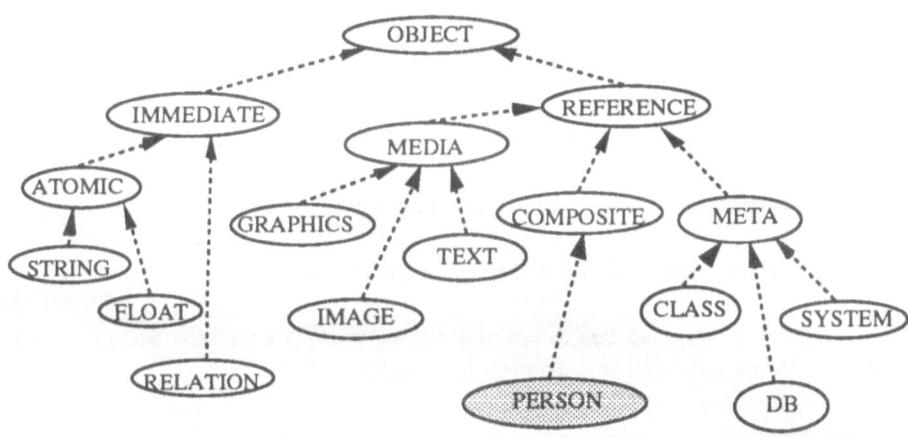

Figure 2.5. Part of a class structure.

META has CLASS as a subclass (See Figure 2.5). CLASS denotes the semantics of class structures. CLASS has attributes such as Super, Kb, Enumerated, and Procedural. CLASS has *dictionary information* such as Relation, Headpid, Tailpid, and Notuple as attributes. CLASS uses the procedural attribute instantiate for class definition. The class ENUMERATED has attributes such as Class, Multiple, Constraint, and If-needed. The class PROCEDURAL has attributes such as Main. PROCEDURAL and ENUMERATED are subclasses of RELATION to be efficiently retrieved without joins. CLASS thus manages classes as usual instances and allows classes to be manipulated as instances. As a subset of META, PROGRAM is defined to manage procedural attributes, demons, and application programs in a uniform fashion. The Jasmine model can manage both datab, or a part of structural knowledge, and programs, or behavioral knowledge. DB, a subset of META, has attributes to manage whole knowledge bases. SYSTEM has attributes to manage sessions and transactions.

2.4 More Formal Semantics

In this section, we restrict our study to the basic part of our database model and propose
its semantics in a more formal way. For example, we eliminate demons and constraints.
We assume the following notions are given:

Di : domains such as INTEGER, FLOAT, STRING, and VSTRING.
D: $U_i\ Di$.
A: a set of attributes.
ID: set of object identifiers.

DEFINITION 1.

We define the notion of *values*.

(1) Every element of D is a value, called an *atomic value*.

(2) Every element of ID is a value, called an *OID value*.

(3) If $v1$, $v2$, ... , vn are values and $A1$, $A2$, ... , An are attributes, then $<A1{:}v1$,
$A2{:}v2$, ... , $An{:}vn>$ is a value, called a *tuple value*.

(4) If $v1$, $v2$, ... , vn are values, then {v1, v2, ... , vn} is a value, called a *set value*.

Note that values here correspond to immediate objects described previously. In
particular, nested tuple values model nested relations, or relation objects.

DEFINITION 2.

We define the notion of *objects*.

(1) A pair (i, v) where i is an OID value and v is an atomic value is an object, called
an *atomic object*.

(2) A pair (i, v) where i is an OID value and v is an OID value is an object, called an
OID object.

(3) A pair (i, v) where i is an OID value and v is a tuple value is an object, called a
tuple object.

(4) A pair (i, v) where i is an OID value and v is a set value is an object, called a *set object*.

Note that objects here correspond to reference objects described previously. On the other hand, values are pseudo objects which have only values and no oids.

DEFINITION 3.

We define the notion of *equalities*.

(1) Two values are equal iff they are identical.

(2) Two objects are equal iff their object identifiers are identical.

Note that if two objects are equal, then their values are equal.

DEFINITION 4.

We define the notion of types. We assume a set of class names.

(1) The name of the domain Di is an *atomic type*.

(2) A class name c is a *reference type*.

(3) If $T1, T2, \ldots , Tn$ are types, then $<A1:T1, A2:T2, \ldots , An:Tn>$ or $<T1, T2, \ldots , Tn>$ is a *tuple type*.

(4) If T is a type, then $\{T\}$ is a *set type*.

Note that set types as components of tuple types model multiple-valued attributes.

DEFINITION 5.

We define the notions of *signatures* and *methods*. We assume a set of method names.

(1) A signature has the following form: $S1, S2, \ldots , Sn \rightarrow S$ where $S1, S2, \ldots , Sn$, and S are types.

(2) A method m is a pair (n, s) where n is a method name and s is a signature $(S1, S2, \ldots , Sn \rightarrow S)$. m is defined on $S1$.

DEFINITION 6.

We define the notion of *interpretations* I associated with types.

(1) $I(Di) = Di$.

(2) $I(c)$ = a function from c to a set of object identifiers.

(3) $I(<A1:T1, A2:T2, \ldots ,An:Tn>) = \{<A1:v1, A2:v2, \ldots , An:vn>|v\ i$ belongs to $I(Ti)$ for $i=1,2, \ldots , n \}$.

(4) $I(\{T\}) = \{\{v1, v2, \ldots , vn\}|vi$ belongs to $I(T)$ for $i=1, 2, \ldots , n\}$.

DEFINITION 7.

We define the notion of *partial order* $<= T$ between two types.

(1) $Di <= T\ Di$.

(2) $c <=T\ c$.

(3) $<A1:T1, A2:T2, \ldots, An:Tn, A\ n+1:T\ n+1, \ldots , A\ m:T\ m> <= T$ $<A1:T'1, A2:T'2, \ldots, A\ n:T'n>$ iff $Ti <= T\ T'i$ for $i = 1, 2, \ldots, n$.

(4) $\{T\} <=T\ \{T'\}$ iff $T <=T\ T'$.

DEFINITION 8.

We define the notion of *partial order* $<=M$ between signatures of two methods m, and m' . Let s $m = (S1, S2, \ldots , Sn \rightarrow S)$ and $sm' = (S'1, S'2, \ldots , S'n \rightarrow S')$.

$sm <= M\ sm'$ iff $Si <=T\ S'\ i$ for $i = 1, 2, \ldots, n$, and $S <= T\ S'$.

DEFINITION 9.

We define the notion of *classes*.

A class is a quadruple (c, T, M, I) where c is a class name, T is a type, M is a set of methods, and I is an interpretation.

DEFINITION 10.

We define the notion of *partial order* $<=$ between two classes (c, T, M, I), and (c', T', M', I').

$c <= c'$ iff

(1) $T <=T \; T'$, and

(2) for each m belonging to M, there exists m' belonging to M' such that m and m' have the same name, and $sm <= M \; sm'$, and

(3) I is included by I'.

The partial order $<=$ models subclass relationships. (1) models attribute type inheritance, (2) models method inheritance, and (3) defines the semantics of subclass relationships.

Chapter 3
DATABASE PROGRAMMING LANGUAGE

This chapter describes an object manipulation language called *Jasmine/C* [ISHI93a] as a *database programming language* which integrates a general-purpose programming language (C) and a database language in an object-oriented context, and which allows the user to program advanced applications. The query language as a database language of Jasmine has the following features different from those of SQL [DATE90] (see Appendix for the complete syntax of a query expression). The semantics can be formally defined through query translation by object operators.

A query consists of target and condition parts. The basic unit of a query expression is an object expression, a class name followed by a series of attribute names. The target part is an object expression, or a list of object expressions. The condition part consists of a logical combination of predicates which compare object expressions. The query returns a set of objects. The object expressions denote object joins, or implicit joins. The object expressions can reference complex objects directly. Nonleaf classes in a class hierarchy can be specified in a query. They are expanded or specialized into the leaf subclasses. Like SQL, explicit joins specified by join predicates are supported by the query language. However, the compared objects are not confined to atomic values. Equality of objects can be tested based on their object identifiers. In that case, the compared classes must be either identical or a superclass and a subclass of a class hierarchy. The object expressions can also contain methods, so the user can manipulate objects set-theoretically and filter a set of objects procedurally. The system-defined methods such as put, delete specified in a query can modify a set of objects. A query can invoke demons which implement integrity facilities introduced by QBE [ZLOO78]. The user can specify multiple-valued attributes in a query. The user can control unnesting of multiple values and apply aggregate functions correctly. Multiple-valued attributes are existentially or universally quantified.

Another important feature for advanced applications is the integration of query and programming facilities. First, the user can specify methods in a query as described above. The user can extend the functionality of the query language just by defining and specifying a method in a query, without modifying the query language processor. The

19

user can develop application programs more compactly without specifying details such as iteration variable declaration and control structures. Making this type of iteration implicit can increase physical data independence [DATE90] of application programs by allowing the system to optimize the query expression.

Second, the user can also define methods by specifying a query for them. This can define so-called virtual attributes and increase logical data independence [DATE90] of application programs when applications evolve.

Third, the fact that the user invokes a query from programs is one of salient aspects of advanced applications. The so-called impedance mismatch problem [DATE90] between the query language and programming language must be solved. We introduce set variables to attain the goal. The set variable has a class defined by an object model as its type and can contain a set of objects returned by a query as its value. The user can fetch an object by sending the scan message to the set variable and operate on the object by sending a dedicated message to the object in an object-oriented programming manner.

Class objects can also be operated set-theoretically for advanced applications. Basic database functions such as transactions, locking, and logging can be provided through system-defined classes. Multimedia data types and operations are provided by implementing them from system-defined primitive classes in a bootstrap manner.

3.1 Set-oriented Access

Set-oriented access allows objects to be associatively operated on. It obtains a set of objects by filtering them using attribute conditions.

3.1.1 Object expressions

The basic unit of set-oriented access is an *object expression*, a class name followed by a series of zero or more attribute names :

> *class*
> *class.attribute-1*
> *class.attribute-1.attribute-2 ...attribute-n*

The object expression *class* denotes a set of instance objects according to the class semantics. The expression *class.attribute-1* denotes a set of instance objects as the attribute value. In general, the object expression evaluates to a set of objects as the values of the last attribute. As attributes are functions, the object expression corresponds to a functional composition which denotes a *functional join* or *implicit join*

[ZANI83] by traversing attributes representing relationships between objects and eliminates the need for join predicates of a relational model in most queries, like the *dot-notation* of GEM [ZANI83]. The object expression allows the user to directly access components of complex objects (*structural access*).

Inherited attributes such as PATIENT.Age and newly-defined attributes such as PATIENT.Height are treated in a uniform fashion. Multiple-valued attributes such as PATIENT.Temperature can be specified like singleton-valued attributes such as PATIENT.Weight. In such cases, the multiple values are normalized into a flat set of objects. This operation corresponds to the *unnest* [ROTH88] operation of nested relations. The enumerated and procedural attributes are treated in the same way to retrieve and manipulate objects associatively unlike the dot-notation of GEM. The system-defined and user-defined attributes are uniformly treated to ease customization of the language. The uniformity described above leads to compact specification of the language.

3.1.2 Queries

Basically, a set-oriented access query has the following form:

> *<target part> where <condition part>*

The target part consists of an object expression, or a list of object expressions. The condition part consists of a logical combination of simple conditions which compare object expressions with comparison operators such as ==, !=, >, >=, <, and <=. The query form evaluates to a set of the target objects satisfying the condition. The elements of the constructed set are objects (OIDs), or values belonging to the database, or newly constructed tuple values. The result type is determined by the query. For example, to find the name and address of a doctor who works in the pediatrics department and is over 45 years of age, the user forms a query as follows:

> (1) [DOCTOR.Name, DOCTOR.Address] where DOCTOR.Dept == "pediatrics"
> and DOCTOR.Age > 45

The tuple operator "[ ]" allows the construction of tuple values. In this case, the tuple operator corresponds to *projection* of relations. Immediate objects are compared by ==, !=, >, >=, <, and <=, based on values.

In general, joins are classified into implicit and explicit joins. Jasmine supports implicit joins as follows:

> (2) DOCTOR.Patient.Age where DOCTOR.Dept == "pediatrics"

This finds the age of patients whom doctors in the pediatrics department are in charge of. Jasmine can also support explicit joins as follows:

(3) [PATIENT.Name, DOCTOR.Name] where PATIENT.Age == DOCTOR.Age
      and PATIENT.Age < 30

This retrieves pairs of names of patients and doctors who are of the same age under 30. Reference objects can be compared by == and != based on OIDs. For example, assume Disease and Specialty are reference attributes (See Figure 3.1):

(4) [PATIENT.Name, DOCTOR.Name] where PATIENT.Condition == "serious"
      and PATIENT.Disease == DOCTOR.Specialty

This query finds the names of serious patients and doctors who specialize in their disease.

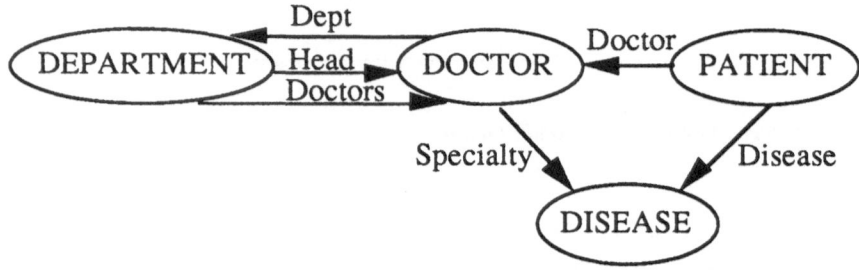

Figure 3.1. Part of a medical database structure.

Multiple-valued attributes are automatically unnested. The following query retrieves a flattened set of temperatures of patients under 13 years of age:

(5) PATIENT.Temperature where PATIENT.Age < 13

Comparison of multiple-valued attributes is interpreted as *at least one* value satisfying the condition, that is, existentially. The following query retrieves the names of patients who ran a temperature of higher than 37.0 degrees centigrade at least once:

(6) PATIENT.Name where PATIENT.Temperature > 37.0

Universally-quantified conditions on multiple attributes can also be specified; this will be described later. Existence of values can be checked by comparison with null as follows:

(7) PATIENT where PATIENT.Disease != null

This finds the OIDs of patients with a known disease. Note that PATIENT is a shortened form of PATIENT.Oid.

There are constraints between several object expressions which appear in one query. If we consider an object model as a graph, then an object expression corresponds to a subgraph. A query is valid only if all subgraphs for object expressions are connected. For example,

(8) PATIENT.Doctor where DOCTOR.Dept == "surgery" (valid)
(9) PATIENT.Doctor where DEPARTMENT == "surgery" (invalid)

The first query is valid because the range class of the attribute Doctor of the class PATIENT is DOCTOR. The second query is invalid because an attribute corresponding to the relationship between DOCTOR and DEPARTMENT is not specified. An object expression can be shortened. For example, if the object expression PATIENT.Doctor appears anywhere in the query and the class of the attribute Doctor of the class PATIENT is DOCTOR, the object expression DOCTOR.Dept has the same value as the expression PATIENT.Doctor.Dept and becomes a shortened form of the latter expression.

The set-oriented query form is similar to an SQL-like language because of its familiarity with the database user. We avoided the introduction of parentheses for nesting queries, unlike SQL for nested relations [ROTH87] and GDL of GENESIS [BATO88]. GemStone [MAIE86], based on Smalltalk-80 [GOLD83], needs to send a *select* message to a collection class to retrieve instances associatively. The Jasmine classes represent sets of objects, eliminating the need for collection classes. And explicit declaration of loop variables is unnecessary unlike DAPLEX [SHIP81]. The user can specify a query compactly.

3.1.3 Incomplete knowledge access

Any class, leaf or nonleaf, in a generalization lattice can be specified in a set-oriented query. According to the interpretation of a class, the intrinsic instances of a nonleaf class and the instances of its subclasses can be retrieved at the same time. For example, to find persons who are older than forty:

(10) PERSON where PERSON.Age > 40

This causes a query be specified compactly because several queries against subclasses such as PATIENT and DOCTOR can be formulated in a single query.

The user can retrieve objects without precise specification. A general class can be specified in a query together with an attribute defined in its subclasses. For example, to find the names of persons who work in the surgery department:

(11) PERSON.Name where PERSON.Dept.Name == "surgery"

The class PERSON is automatically specialized to the subclass DOCTOR with the attribute Dept defined. In the extreme case, OBJECT can be used in a query. This mechanism fits with how we define some concepts by differentiating a general concept by providing specializing attributes. The user can thus formulate a query without knowing specificity like a natural language query. The translation from a natural language query to a Jasmine query would be straightforward if we adopt Jasmine as the target system of a natural language front-end [ISHI87].

The user can impose a condition on the categorization attribute of a general class with a partition. If the specified condition matches some of the categorization conditions of the partition, the specified class can be specialized to some of the partition members. For example, to find persons who are younger than thirteen:

(12) PERSON where PERSON.Age < 13

The class PERSON is automatically specialized to CHILD.

Of course, the user can retrieve only intrinsic instances of a nonleaf class by specifying the name of the nonleaf class in a condition on the Class attribute. For example, to find the names of persons who live in Tokyo and are neither a doctor nor a patient and whose age is unknown:

(13) PERSON.Name where PERSON.Class == <PERSON>
                          and   PERSON.Address == "Tokyo"

This allows the user to manipulate only incomplete knowledge, that is, intrinsic instances of PERSON. Note that the bracketed class name denotes the class itself (See Section 3.5.1). Thus, the ability to flexibly access incomplete knowledge differentiates Jasmine from other systems such as [FISH87].

3.1.4 Set-oriented operation

A set-oriented query is not restricted to only retrieval. The user can do operations other than retrieval in the set-oriented access by using procedural attributes, which can be specified in any part of an attribute of an object expression of a query. The additional parameters of the procedural attribute are given in parentheses:

  class.attr.procedural-attribute(parml , parm2)

Several procedural attributes can appear in one object expression like this:

  class.procedural-attribute-1(parml).procedural-attribute-2(parm2)

For example, to make and display a copy of serious patients' medical certificates dated January 8, 1989, the user formulates the following query:

  (14) PATIENT.make-medical-certificate("19890108").display()
       where PATIENT.Condition == "serious"

Assuming that we operate on objects set-theoretically in a setting other than Jasmine, we then have to retrieve a set of objects and scan and operate on each object in an iteration construct. In contrast, Jasmine makes this type of iteration implicit and iteration variable declaration unnecessary and allows the user to compactly specify a query without knowing the details. This increases productivity in application development. Implicit iteration would allow the compiler to easily translate from serial to concurrent access of objects in a multi-processor context when it is possible.

Of course, we can also specify procedural attributes in incomplete knowledge access. If we specify a general class whose subclasses have procedural attributes of the same name which have different implementations, the different attributes are invoked in a single query at the same time. For example, to display heterogeneous media objects such as images, graphics, created January 8, 1989 at the same time, the user specifies the following query:

  (15) MEDIA.display() where MEDIA.Date == "19890108"

The system-defined and user-defined procedural attributes can be specified in the same way unlike other systems such as [FISH87]. For example, the user can print interns who work in the surgery department by use of the system-defined print:

  (16) DOCTOR.print( ) where DOCTOR.Dept.Name == "surgery"
                         and DOCTOR.Status == "internship"

The system-defined attributes include object modification operations such as put, replace, delete, and destroy. They can be invoked in a set-oriented query. For example, the following query adds 36.5 degrees centigrade to James' temperature (multiple-valued attribute):

(17) PATIENT.put("Temperature", 36.5) where PATIENT.Name == "James Bond"

The following query replaces *all* the values of the attribute Temperature of patients in a good condition by null:

(18) PATIENT.replace("Temperature", null) where PATIENT.Condition == "good"

The following removes *only* the doctor denoted by the variable *drno* from the multiple-valued attribute Doctor of the surgery department.

(19) DEPARTMENT.delete("Doctor", drno) where DEPARTMENT.Name == "surgery"

The user can replace *one* particular value of multiple-valued attributes by combining delete and put. The following fires Dr.No.

(20) DOCTOR.destroy() where DOCTOR.Name == "Dr. No"

Instantiation, creation of an instance, is done by a class procedural attribute described in Section 3.5.1. The fact that we make no distinction between the system-defined and user-defined attributes in a query means that the user can customize the object manipulation language without changing the language processor. The user can extend the functions of the object manipulation language just by adding the user-defined procedural attributes.

3.1.5 Aggregate functions and set functions

Aggregate functions, attributes taking a set of objects and giving a singleton can be specified in a set-oriented query. They include the system-defined attributes such as count, average, sum, max, and min. Since a set in our context allows duplication of objects, the user can use the aggregate functions naturally. For example, to find the number of patients who are over 45 years of age, the user forms a query as follows:

(21) PATIENT.count() where PATIENT.Age > 45

The following query finds the average of the ages of serious patients,

(22) PATIENT.Age.average() where PATIENT.Condition == "serious"

If the user needs to convert a bag to a set in the strict sense, the user can do that by using the set function unique:

(23) PATIENT.Age.unique().average() where PATIENT.Condition == "serious"

In general, the aggregate functions take as input the whole flattened set retrieved just before the function evaluation. This causes subtle problems when the user applies the aggregate functions to the multiple-valued attribute. Assuming that the attribute Temperature is a multiple-valued attribute, consider the following:

(24) PATIENT.Temperature.average() where PATIENT.Condition == "serious"

This evaluates to the average of a automatically normalized set of objects as the values of Temperature of more than one serious patient. Therefore, if the user wants to apply the average to Temperature values of each PATIENT object, the user specifies a special operator "{}" to prohibit automatic unnesting of multiple-valued attributes. Then the correct expression is as follows:

(25) PATIENT.{Temperature}.average() where PATIENT.Condition == "serious"

Further, the user can get the maximum of the averages like this:

(26) PATIENT.{Temperature}.average().max()
     where PATIENT.Condition == "serious"

Universally-quantified conditions on multiple-valued attributes can be specified by use of the operators "{}" and "All" as follows:

(27) PATIENT.Name where PATIENT.{Temperature} All> 37.0

This retrieves the names of patients whose temperature is higher than 37.0 degrees centigrade all day long.

We also provide the *group by* clause like relational database systems. The following query retrieves a set of the average temperature of serious patients of the same age:

(28) PATIENT.Temperature.average() where PATIENT.Condition == "serious"
     groupby PATIENT.Age

And the set functions take and give a set of objects, not singletons. They include union, intersection, difference, unique, and sort. For example,

(29) PATIENT.sort("Age").print() where PATIENT.Condition == "serious"

This prints the qualified patients after sorting them by the attribute Age.

3.1.6 Procedural attributes in conditions

Procedural attributes can also be specified in object expressions in the condition part of a query. They are used to filter objects procedurally. This is powerful in a variety of applications. A content-based search of multimedia data can be done by defining a dedicated attribute like (See Section 3.4) as follows:

    (30) XRAY.Patient where XRAY.like(sample-1) == true

This finds a patient whose X-ray looks like sample-1 containing some disease. When the user needs to define the meaning of a modifier such as adjectives in a natural language interface, the user can define the modifier as an attribute and use it in the condition of a query as the meaning of the natural language query. For example, an adjective *critical* (See Section 3.4) is defined and specified:

    (31) PATIENT.Doctor where PATIENT.critical() == true

This means the natural language query "Let me know the doctors in charge of serious patients." Condition attributes are usually defined to take an object and give a Boolean value, true or false. The user can also specify aggregate functions in conditions as follows:

    (32) PATIENT.Name where PATIENT.{Temperature}.average() < 37.0

This finds the name of a patient whose temperature average is below 37.0 degrees centigrade.

Procedural attributes both in the target part and in the condition part are compiled to directly access objects in database buffers, as described later. This eliminates the need for transferring unnecessary data from the buffer to application programs and executes the application programs more efficiently than conventional approaches.

3.1.7 Demons

If demons, such as if-added and if-needed, are attached to attributes specified in object expressions of a query, they are invoked by associated events such as if-added and if-needed. The events are triggered by the invocation of procedural attributes such as put and by the reference of enumerated attributes such as Height. The actions invoked after events happen, such as the if-added demon of Condition of PATIENT (See Section 3.4), are defined like a procedural attribute. This mechanism can flexibly realize active databases containing triggers and alerters unlike other systems such as [FISH87]. For example,

(33) PATIENT.put("Condition", "serious") where PATIENT.Name == "James Bond"

This query invokes the action of giving a notice to the head of the department of James' doctor that James' condition has gotten serious. Similarly, change notification associated with CAD applications can be achieved by using demons. Demons can also propagate updates in a component object of a complex object to other components or the whole object to maintain internal consistency among them [ISHI90]. Whether demons are actually invoked or not is controlled by the user with an option. If the user specifies the no-demon option, no demon is invoked even after associated events happen. No extra codes for demon invocation are generated, so there is no overhead.

3.2 More Formal Semantics

3.2.1 Object operators

We introduce our basic object operators through which the semantics of queries can be defined. In general, operators have names and signatures as follows:

selector: *object, parameter 1, ... , parameter n -> object'*

Object is a type for a receiver object [STEF86]. *Selector* is the name of a method defined on *object*. *Parameter i* is a type for *i* th parameter for the method. *Object'* is a type for result objects. In particular, *object* and *object* ' are set types. This construct sends *object* a message consisting of *selector* and *parameter i* ($i=1,2, ... ,n$) and gets *object'* as the result.

We assume the following symbols are given: S, T, U, V, Si, Ti, and Vi denote object types; s, t, u, v, si, ti, and v denote instance objects. A, A , and A' denote attribute names; a, ai, and a' denote attribute values; f, g, fi, and gi denote methods; and af denotes aggregate functions. P denotes logical combination of conditions on singleton-valued attributes with no methods, no multiple-valued attributes, no aggregate functions, and no series of attributes. *Pjoin* denotes join predicates. *BOOLEAN* denotes the type of a set object {true, false}. LUB denotes the least upper bound of two types. GLB denotes the greatest lower bound of two types. We define the basic object operators by giving their signatures and semantics.

project
(1) project: $\{<A1:T1, A2:T2, \ldots, An:Tn, An+1:Tn+1, \ldots, Am:Tm>\}$, $(A1, A2, \ldots, An) \to \{<A1:T1, A2:T2, \ldots, An:Tn>\}$
(2) project $(S, (A1, A2, \ldots, An)) = \{<a1, a2, \ldots, an> \mid s$ belongs to S and ai is the value of Ai of $s\}$

This operator projects attributes of tuples.

project-apply
(1) project-apply: $\{T\}, (A1, (f1:T \to T1), A2, (f2:T \to T2), \ldots, An, (fn:T \to Tn)) \to \{<A1:T1, A2:T2, \ldots, An:Tn>\}$
(2) project-apply$(S, (A1, f1, A2, f2, \ldots, An, fn)) = \{<A1:f1 (s), A2:f2(s), \ldots, An:fn(s)> \mid s$ belongs to $S\}$

This operator constructs tuples whose components are the results of functions applied to elements of an input set.

restrict
(1) restrict: $\{T\}, (P:T \to BOOLEAN) \to \{T\}$
(2) restrict$(S, P) = \{s \mid s$ belongs to S and $P(s)\}$

This operator returns a set of tuples satisfying a predicate.

restrict-apply
(1) restrict-apply: $\{T\}, A, (f:T \to U), (g:T \to BOOLEAN), (P:T \to BOOLEAN) \to \{<T, A:U>\}$
(2) restrict-apply$(S, A, f, g, P) = \{<s, A:f(s)> \mid s$ belongs to S and $g(s)$ and $P(s)\}$

This operator constructs tuples consisting of an element of an input set and the result of a function applied to the element satisfying a predicate and a function predicate.

join
(1) join: $\{T\}, \{U\}, (Pjoin:T,U \to BOOLEAN) \to \{<T, U>\}$
(2) join$(S1, S2, Pjoin) = \{<s1, s2> \mid s1$ belongs to $S1$ and $s2$ belongs to $S2$ and $Pjoin(s1, s2)\}$

This operator constructs new tuples from tuples of two input sets satisfying a join predicate.

join-apply
(1) join-apply: $\{T\}, \{U\}, A1, (f1:T \to V1), (g1:T \to BOOLEAN), A2, (f2:U \to V2), (g2:U \to BOOLEAN), (Pjoin:T, U \to BOOLEAN) \to \{<T, U, A1:V1, A2:V2>\}$

(2) join-apply($S1$, $S2$, $A1$, $f1$, $g1$, $A2$, $f2$, $g2$, $Pjoin$) = {<$s1$, $s2$, $A1$:$f1(s1)$, $A2$:$f2(s2)$>| $s1$ belongs to $S1$ and $s2$ belongs to $S2$ and $g1(s1)$ and $g2(s2)$ and $Pjoin(s1,$ $s2)$}

This operator constructs tuples from elements of two input sets and the results of functions applied to the elements satisfying a join predicate and function predicates applied to the elements.

aggregate
(1) aggregate: {<$A1$:$T1$, $A2$:$T2$, ... , A:{T}, ..., An:Tn>}, A, (af:{T} -> U), A'
-> {<$A1$:$T1$, $A2$:$T2$, ..., A:{T}, ... , An:Tn, A':U>}
(2) aggregate(S, A, af, A') = {<s, A':$af(a)$>|s belongs to S and a is the value of A of s}

This operator constructs tuples whose components are elements of an input set and the results of an aggregate function applied to a multiple-valued attribute of the elements.

aggregate-singleton
(1) aggregate-singleton: {T }, (af:{T } -> U) -> {U}
(2) aggregate-singleton(S,af) = {$af(S)$}

This operator takes a set and returns the result of an aggregate function applied to the set.

flatten
(1) flatten: {{T }} -> {T }
(2) flatten(S) = {t | s belongs to S and t belongs to s}

This operator takes a set of sets of tuples and returns a set of tuples.

nest
(1) nest: {<$A1$:$T1$, $A2$:$T2$, ..., A:T, ... , An:Tn>}, A -> {<A 1:$T1$, $A2$:$T2$, ... , A:{T}, ... , An:Tn>}
(2) nest(S, A) = {<$a1$, $a2$, ... , a' , ... , an> | For each a belonging to a', there exists s such that s belongs to A and ai is the value of Ai of s and a is the value of A of s }

This operator nests tuples along attributes other than the specified ones.

unnest
(1) unnest: {<$A1$:$T1$, $A2$:$T2$, ... , A:{T}, ... , An:Tn>}, A
-> {<$A1$:$T1$, $A2$:$T2$, ... , A:T, ... , An:Tn>}

(2) unnest$(S, A) = \{<a1, a2, ... , a', ... , an> \mid s$ belongs to S and a_i is the value of A_i of s and a is the value of A of s and a' belongs to $a\}$

This operator unnests tuples along specified attributes.

eliminate
(1) eliminate: $\{T\} \rightarrow \{T\}$
(2) eliminate$(S) = \{u \mid$ there exists only one u such that s belongs to S and $u = s\}$
This operator eliminates duplicates of elements from a set, based on equalities.

union
(1) union: $\{T\}, \{U\} \rightarrow \{V\}$ where $V = \text{LUB}(T, U)$
(2) union$(S1, S2) = \{v \mid v$ belongs to $S1$ or v belongs to $S2\}$

This operator returns union of two input sets.

difference
(1) difference: $\{T\}, \{U\} \rightarrow \{T\}$
(2) difference$(S1, S2) = \{s1 \mid s1$ belongs to $S1$ and $s1$ does not belong to $S2\}$

This operator returns the difference of two input sets.

intersection
(1) intersection: $\{T\}, \{U\} \rightarrow \{V\}$ where $V = \text{GLB}(T, U)$
(2) intersection$(S1, S2) = \{v \mid v$ belongs to $S1$ and v belongs to $S2\}$

This operator returns the intersection of two input sets.

Note that the above operators are not necessarily minimal but sufficient for describing query semantics. For example, the operator restrict can be simulated by specifying *none* parameters as methods in the operator restrict-apply.

3.2.2 Query semantics

Now we describe the semantics of queries through translation, using the above described object operators. We assume the following symbols are given: C, $C1$, and $C2$ denote class names. A, $A1$, $A2$, and $A3$ denote attribute names. *Oid* denotes the name of the attribute containing object identifiers. *Method* denotes method names and *aggfunc* denotes aggregate function names. P, $P1$, and $P2$ denote logical combination of conditions on singleton-valued attributes with no multiple-valued attributes, no methods, and no aggregate functions. *Pjoin* denotes join predicates; *none* denotes absence of parameters; v denotes constants; and * denotes all the attributes of an object.

We define semantic translation rules for queries in a pattern-directed fashion.

singleton-valued attributes, methods, and aggregate functions
(1) *C.A* where *P* -> project(restrict(*C*, *P*), (*A*))
(2) *C.method* where *P* -> project(restrict-apply(*C*, *A*, *method*, *none*, *P*), (*A*))
(3) *C.aggfunc* where *P* -> aggregate-singleton(restrict(*C*, *P*), *aggfunc*)

multiple-valued attributes, and methods
(4) *C.A* where *P* -> project(restrict(unnest(*C*, *A*), *P*), (*A*))
(5) *C.method* where *P* -> flatten(project(restrict-apply(*C*, *A*, *method*, *none*, *P*), (*A*)))

a series of singleton-valued attributes
(6) *C.A1.A2* where *P* -> project(join(restrict(*C*, *P*), *C1*, *A1=Oid*), (*A2*))
where *C1* denotes the class name for the range of *A1* and *Oid* denotes the attribute name for OID of *C1*.

a series of methods
(7) *C.method1.method2* where *P*
-> project-apply(project(join(restrict-apply(*C*, *A1*, *method1*, *none*, *P*), *C1*, *A1=Oid*), (*)), (*A2*, *method2*))
where *C1* denotes the class name for the range of *method1* and *Oid* denotes the attribute name for OID of *C1* and * denotes all the attributes of *C1*.

a series of singleton-valued attributes and aggregate functions
(8) *C.A.aggfunc* where *P*
-> aggregate-singleton(project(restrict(*C*, *P*), (*A*)), *aggfunc*)

a series of multiple-valued attributes and aggregate functions
(9) *C.A.aggfunc* where *P* -> aggregate-singleton(flatten(project(restrict(*C*, *P*), (*A*))), *aggfunc*)
(10) *C.{A}.aggfunc* where *P*
-> project(aggregate(restrict(*C*, *P*), *A*, *aggfunc*, *A1*), (*A1*))

group by
(11) *C.A.aggfunc* where *P* groupby *C.A1*
-> project(aggregate(nest(project(restrict(*C*, *P*), (*A*, *A1*)), *A*), *A*, *aggfunc*, *A2*), (*A2*))

multiple targets
(12) [*C.A1*, *C.A2*] where *P* -> project(restrict(*C*, *P*), (*A1*, *A2*))
(13) [*C1.A 1*, *C 2.A2*] where *Pjoin* and *P1* and *P2*
-> project(join(restrict(*C1*, *P1*), restrict(*C2*, *P2*), *Pjoin*), (*A1*, *A2*))
(14) [*C.A1*, *C.A2.A3*] where *P* -> project(join(restrict(*C*, *P*), *C2*, *A2=Oid*), (*A1*, *A3*))

where *C2* denotes the class name for the range of *A2* and *Oid* denotes the attribute name for OID of *C2*.

(15) [*C.A, C.method*] where *P*   -> project(restrict-apply(*C, A1, method, none, P*), (*A, A 1*))

(16) [*C.method1, C.method2*] where *P* -> project-apply(restrict(*C, P*), (*A1, method1, A2, method2*))

(17) [*C1.method1, C2.method2*] where *P join* and *P1* and *P2*
-> project(join-apply(restrict(*C1, P1*), restrict(*C2, P2*), *A1, method1, none, A2, method2, none, Pjoin*), (*A1, A2*))

methods in conditions
(18) *C.A* where *C.method*==true and *P*
-> project(restrict-apply(*C, A1, none, method, P*), (*A*))

multiple-valued attributes in conditions
(19) *C.A* where *C.A1*=*v* and *P* -> project(restrict(unnest(restrict(*C, P*), *A1*), *A 1=v*), (*A*))

aggregate functions in conditions
(20) *C.A* where *C.{A1}.aggfunc*=*v* and *P*
-> project(restrict(aggregate(restrict(*C, P*), *A1, aggfunc, A2*), *A2=v*), (*A*))

universally-quantified conditions on multiple-valued attributes
(21) *C.A* where *C.{A1}* All== *v* and *P*
-> project(restrict(aggregate(restrict(*C, P*), *A1*, All= (*v*), *A2*), *A2*=true), (*A*))

a series of attributes in conditions
(22) *C.A* where *C.A1.A2*=*v* and *P*
-> project(join(restrict(*C, P*), restrict(*C1, A2=v*), *A 1=Oid*), (*A*))

where *C1* denotes the class name for the range of *A1* and *Oid* denotes the attribute name for OID of *C1*.

The semantics of the example queries (1) - (33) described earlier can be defined by applying one of the above rules directly. Those of the rest, such as (16), (23), (24) can be defined by combining some of the rules. For example, if we replace "restrict(*C, P*)" in rule (22) by "restrict-apply(*C, A, method, none, P*)" in rule (2), we can describe the semantics of query (16).

Similarly, we can describe semantic translation rules for queries with more complicated expressions such as a series of more than two attributes, and a target list of more than two object expressions. We provide the following rules to reduce such complicated expressions to less complicated ones. To reduce a series of more than two attributes in the target part, we use "join(restrict(*C*, *P*), *C1*, *A1=Oid*)" instead of "restrict(*C*, *P*)" in rule (6). Similarly, to reduce a series of more than two attributes in the condition part, we use "join(restrict(*C*, *P*), *C1*, *A1=Oid*)" instead of "restrict(*C*, *P*)" in rule (22). For a target list of more than two expressions, we use "project((*A1*, *A2*))" instead of "project((*A1*))" in rule (12). Generally, logical operations on the above conditions such as "and" and "or" lead to set operations on queries such as "intersection" and "union", although simple conjunction of the conditions can be described by merging the above rules. Note that the above rules are not necessarily optimal.

3.3 Singleton Access and Object Variables

In the previous section we described set-oriented access of objects. To individually process objects is also necessary for application programming and procedural attribute definition. This type of access is called *singleton access* in contrast to set-oriented access. Jasmine can do both set-oriented and singleton access of objects embedded in a general-purpose programming language C. This differentiates Jasmine from other systems such as DAPLEX [SHIP81] and IRIS [FISH87].

It is important to individually access a set of retrieved objects. That necessitates a variable which can be bound to a set of objects. The variable is called a *set variable*. The set variable is usually set to the result of a set-oriented query. The user can access objects one by one by scanning the set variable. The *instance variable* is also introduced to hold a singleton. The instance variable holds an object like usual variables in a conventional programming language. The instance variable and set variable constitute the object variable. The object variable integrates set-oriented access of a database system and singleton access of a programming language. The existence of a *multiple* option at declaration determines whether the object variable is a set variable. For example,

      PATIENT ps multiple, p;

ps and *p* are declared as set variable and instance variable of PATIENT type. In general, the set variable is set to the result set of a set-oriented query at the right-hand side of a statement. The user can access objects individually by using the system-defined procedural attributes as follows:

```
ps = PATIENT where PATIENT.Age >= 10;
ps.openscan();
while (p = ps.next())
   { ... }
ps.closescan();
```

The procedural attribute *next* returns an object at each invocation, which is set to the instance variable p for further use.

The object variable can be specified in an object expression in place of a class name. For example,

    p.Doctor.Name = "Dr.No";
    n = p.Doctor.Dept.Name;

The object expression at the right-hand side of a statement is referenced. The object expression at the left-hand side is modified by the right-hand side value. Modification in singleton access is done by this.

If demons are defined in the attribute and the demon option is chosen, they are invoked by triggering events. The reference of the object expression invokes an if-needed demon if the attribute has a null value. If the if-needed demon is invoked, the object expression evaluates to the result of the demon like a default value. For example,

    h=p.Height;

If the value of Height is unknown, the if-needed demon of Height computes its value from the value of Weight. The modification of the object expression invokes either an if-added, if-updated, or if-removed demon depending whether the attribute is inserted, changed, or deleted. The constraint demon is used to dynamically check the type of the right-hand side value which cannot be statically determined by the compiler. Assume the attribute Weight has the constraint of being positive:

    p.Weight = scales();

If invalidation of the constraint occurs, for example, if the scales return a negative number for some reason, the modification is inhibited.

The procedural attributes can also be specified in the object expression as follows:

    p.make-medical-certificate("19890210").print();
    p.make-medical-certificate("19890210").Size="A4";
    tavg=p.Temperature.average();

If demons are attached to the procedural attribute, they are invoked with the demon option. These object expressions are an extension of a *message sending statement* [STEF86] of a conventional object-oriented programming language such as C++ [STRO86].

The object expression including set variables or multiple-valued attributes evaluates to a set of objects. Thus, the result is set to a set variable. Assume that Temperature is multiple-valued:

```
STRING ns multiple;
FLOAT ts multiple;

ns = ps.Name;
ts = p.Temperature;
```

Conditions can be also specified as follows:

```
ns = ps.Name where ps.Age < 3;
ts = p.Temperature where p.Temperature > 37.0;
```

Access of the set variable is done by the system-defined procedural attributes in the same way as set-oriented access. The modification of the multiple-valued attribute is done by the system-defined attributes such as put, delete, replace. If the result of a set-oriented query is known to be a singleton in advance or the first element of the result set is only concerned, the instance variable is used instead. Of course, the application of the aggregate functions such as average evaluates to a singleton.

3.4 Procedural Attribute and Demon Definition

The user can basically define a procedural attribute by using singleton access as follows:

```
class
  Procedural class1 procedural-attribute (p1, p2)
    class1 result;
    type1 p1;
    type2 p2;
    { ...self.attr ...
        return result; }
```

The function range class is *class1* and variables *p1* and *p2* are parameters given to the procedural-attribute. The system-defined instance variable self is bound to the instance of the class where this procedural attribute is defined. self corresponds to a receiver object. The procedural attribute body can include set-oriented access, singleton access, and a general-purpose programming language C as well. The procedural attribute definition takes maximum advantage of the object manipulation language Jasmine/C. The procedural attribute invocation is just done by its reference in an object expression as described previously.

The concept of *derivation* [SHIP81] [HAMM81] is needed to accommodate conceptual abstraction and user views. Jasmine procedural attributes can define such derivation generally in Jasmine/C, not confined to the special constructs as DAPLEX introduces [SHIP81]. While IRIS classifies functions into *stored, derived, foreign*, and *compound functions* [FISH87], Jasmine integrates the last three types into one type procedural.

We describe user-defined procedural attributes referenced in the previous examples. The procedural attribute make-medical-certificate is defined in Figure 2.1 The following procedural attribute defined in the class PHOTO which has XRAY as a subclass does the content-based searching using existing programs:

> Procedural BOOLEAN like (p)
>   PHOTO p;
>   { return (partial-match (self, p)) }

The following procedural attribute in PATIENT defines the adjective critical as conceptual abstraction:

> Procedural BOOLEAN critical()
>   { if (self.Condition == "serious" && self.Room == "ICU")
>   return true }

Procedural attributes can include set-oriented queries. The following attribute of the class DEPARTMENT defines interns who work in a department:

> Procedural DOCTOR intern()
>   { self.Doctor where self.Doctor.Status == "internship" }

This can be specified in a query to retrieve interns in the surgery department as follows:

> DEPARTMENT.intern() where DEPARTMENT.Name == "surgery"

This can simulate nesting of queries.

A demon is also defined like a procedural attribute. For example, the following demon in the attribute Condition of PATIENT defines a function which notifies the Department head that a patient's condition is becoming serious.

Enumerated STRING Condition if-added
{ if (value == "serious") notify(self.Doctor.Dept.Head, self.Name) }

Demons have no explicit parameters except the system-defined instance variables such as self and value and they are implicitly invoked by their associated events caused by modification functions.

The programs, whether applications, procedural attributes, or demons, are explicitly managed by PROGRAM objects, which have enumerated attributes such as source, binary, and procedural attributes such as compile, and link. In other words, the whole knowledge-based application can be defined in Jasmine/C.

3.5   Miscellaneous   Operations

3.5.1 Class operations

A class is modeled by the system-defined class CLASS as described previously. Classes and instances are accessed in a uniform fashion. Classes have *class procedural attributes* which operate on classes themselves. They include the attributes such as instantiate and destroy. A particular class is specified by bracketing the class name in an object expression. For example,

<PATIENT>.instantiate(Weight 65.5);

This invokes the instantiate attribute of REFERENCE, a superclass of PATIENT, and creates an instance of PATIENT. The mandatory attribute Weight is supplied the value. The user can create a class similarly.

<CLASS>.instantiate(DOCTOR Db MEDICINE Super PERSON ...);

This invokes the instantiate attribute of CLASS and creates the class DOCTOR. The class is destroyed by the following object expression:

<DOCTOR>.destroy();

This invokes the destroy attribute of REFERENCE.

Classes can be associatively retrieved like instances:

CLASS.print() where CLASS.Enumerated.Class == <DOCTOR>

The above query prints classes which have DOCTOR as the range class of enumerated attributes. This helps greatly as a *data dictionary* when the user makes a query. It is also important when the user defines a new class by modifying existent classes. As the application evolves, the user often has to define a new class not from scratch, but from existing classes. For example, the user of a CAD system retrieves a large library of design solutions represented by classes and modifies these designs to satisfy the given specifications. Other systems such as [FISH87] lack this ability to flexibly manipulate generic knowledge.

3.5.2 Database operations

The system-defined classes SYSTEM and DB have attributes responsible for database operations. This abstracts database operations such as session and transaction management as objects and provides database amenities [MAIE86]. The class DB has enumerated attributes such as Lock and Log, and procedural attributes such as open, close, and destroy for database management. The class SYSTEM has enumerated attributes such Nobuf, Nodb, Transaction and procedural attributes such as open, close, begintransaction, endtransaction, and restoretransaction. For example, the skeleton of a typical database session is represented as follows:

```
main ()
{
system.open();
db1.open();
system.begintransaction();
...
   object access
...
system.endtransaction();
db1.close();
system.close();
}
error()
{if (system.Transaction == open) system.restoretransaction();}
```

This makes the system status and operations explicit enough for the user to inspect and control.

3.5.3   Multimedia operations

We provide basic multimedia support needed by new applications. Multimedia include images, graphics, and text. The class IMAGE has attributes such as header information, Frame, and Pixel. The header information describes additional attributes of images. The attribute Frame contains bulk data in secondary memory. The attribute Pixel contains pixel data allocated continuously in main memory. IMAGE has procedural attributes such as input, output, display, move and change-size. The user builds the functions necessary for the applications by combining these basic attributes, but not from scratch.

GRAPHICS objects consist of PRIMITIVE objects, which have attributes such as relative address-based data and absolute address-based data. PRIMITIVE is classified into LINE, CIRCLE, POLYGON, and so forth. The relative data is used for describing graphics data. The absolute data is translated from the relative data and is used for actual display. The procedural attributes for GRAPHICS also include input, output, display, move, and change-size. TEXT objects have attributes such as string data for storage and graphics text data for display. The TEXT procedural attributes also include input, output, display, move, and change-size. TEXT objects can contain other arbitrary objects as subtexts.

IMAGE, GRAPHICS, and TEXT have the same interface for the same manipulation such as move although each implementation differs from one to another. Consider the following object expression:

MEDIA m;
m.move( );

This expression can apply to images, graphics, and text. If the instance variable m is bound to an IMAGE instance, the move attribute of IMAGE is invoked. If m is bound to a GRAPHICS instance, the move of GRAPHICS is selected. This media polymorphism increases the availability of application programs.

MEDIA objects which will be displayed are managed by the class FIGURE which has the class ARRANGEMENT as multiple-valued attributes. ARRANGEMENT objects have MEDIA objects and their locations. FIGURE is a subclass of MEDIA, so FIGURE objects can be arbitrarily nested. WINDOW objects display a part or whole of a FIGURE object. Heterogeneous media can be displayed by overlapping in one window. The user defines FIGURE objects to develop multimedia applications. Direct manipulation of displayed multimedia data is important. Direct manipulation of displayed multimedia data can be done by clicking the displayed object and invoking its procedural attributes. Objects contained by displayed text can also be directly accessed by clicking. We have confirmed the feasibility of Jasmine as a next generation hypermedia engine which enables complex object modeling and flexible searching in addition to link traversal [ISHI90].

3.5.4 Persistent objects and temporary objects

We described objects stored in a database of secondary memory. They are called *persistent objects*. In contrast, Jasmine can also treat volatile objects as a conventional expert shell or object-oriented programming language handles. They are called *temporary objects*. The user can define the class for temporary objects by supplying the option at class definition. Jasmine can be then used as a conventional expert shell or object-oriented programming language. The user can use temporary and persistent objects almost uniformly. Naturally, temporary objects can be more efficiently accessed. In addition, the user can load a part of persistent objects into programs at compilation. They are efficiently treated as temporary objects at execution without using the database. Both instances and classes can be loaded in advance associatively by using a subset of the object manipulation language. For example,

    instance PATIENT where PATIENT.Condition == "serious";

This loads PATIENTs whose conditions are serious in advance at compilation. This ability is appropriate for CAD simulations.

Chapter 4
IMPLEMENTATION

First, we will discuss the system architecture consisting of two subsystems, the data management subsystem and the object management subsystem. The data management subsystem is an extended relational database kernel called *XRDB*. It is used to efficiently store and access objects in secondary memory. The object management subsystem supports the object model and the object manipulation language on top of the data management subsystem. We will explain the function and implementation of the data management subsystem, and the storage of objects and implementation of the object manipulation language using this subsystem.

The Jasmine architecture consists of the data management and object management subsystems for flexibility. The data management subsystem supports nested relations and their operations. Simple data structures, such as relations and tuples, hash-based operations, such as hash join and set-difference, and a variety of user-defined functions, such as manipulation and predicate functions, enable efficient database processing. Basic facilities, such as transactions, concurrency control, and recovery, are supported by this subsystem. The object management subsystem stores objects efficiently by using nested relations. This subsystem processes queries efficiently by query optimization and accesses in-memory objects efficiently by object buffering. We summarize the features of the implementation focusing on data management, object storage, query optimization, and object buffering as follows.

(1) Data management

The data management subsystem provides only relations (sequential, B-tree, hash, and inner relations). A B-tree relation is a clustered index in itself. A non-clustered index can be constructed by storing only keys and TIDs (tuple identifiers) in B-tree or hash relations. Hash relations are based on linear hashing with partial expansion [LARS80]. Inner relations are implemented by storing them in variable-length fields of tuples. Nested relations are realized by recursively storing inner relations in fields of another

43

inner relation.

The data management subsystem supports only fixed-length and variable-length data as field data types. The subsystem makes no interpretation of field values except for TIDs and inner relations. Tuples consist of fixed and variable parts. Fixed-length fields and offsets of variable-length fields are stored in the fixed part. Variable-length fields are stored in the variable part. Any field can be accessed in a constant time. To avoid unnecessary data movement, the subsystem uses pointer arrays to access tuples for internal processing such as internal sorting and hashing, and uses pointer arrays to access fields on the page buffers.

Joins are processed by a nested-loop join, a TID join, or a hash join method. The hash join method uses the internal hash join, which is recursion- and partition-free, if either of two input relations for joins can be entirely loaded into buffers. Otherwise, the external hash join is used, which recursively partitions relations into subrelations and applies the internal hash join as a special case.

The data management subsystem allows the user of the subsystem to specify application-specific parts by providing user-defined functions. They include manipulation and predicate functions for section or join operators, order and range functions for index insertion and search, and hash functions for hash-based operators such as hash join and set-difference.

The data management subsystem provides no query parser or optimizer. It is just an executer of three-level operators: relational operators, tuple operators, and storage operators. All these operators are open to the user. The relational operators extend relational algebra by allowing the user to operate on nested relations and to specify user-defined functions.

Transactions in the data management subsystem are atomic and serializable. Concurrency control is based on granularity, two-phase locking. Deadlock is detected by analyzing the Wait-For-Graph of transactions. Recovery uses shadow-paging.

(2)Object storage

The object management subsystem uses nested relations rather than flat relations to efficiently store nested structures of objects unlike other systems. Multiple values are stored in multiple-valued fields, the simplest form of nested relations. Object identifiers are stored into a database with almost no conversion because they are logical. Only the inspection of an object identifier of an object can determine the class to which the object belongs, without the overhead of retrieving the content of the object. Inherited and non-inherited attributes are concatenated into one tuple, which can avoid the partition overhead.

Property and method definitions, inherently nested, specified in a class are stored in nested relations. Programs such as methods and demons are stored as objects in a database. They are retrieved and used by query optimization. Heterogeneous classes are stored in a database, which enables flexible queries against classes.

(3) Query optimization

The object management subsystem performs query optimization by two steps. The first step translates a user query into a canonical form called a query graph, a subgraph of an object model. The second step takes the query graph and generates an optimal access plan of extended relational operators. Query optimization in an object-oriented database system has features different from those of query optimization in a relational database system, as follows. First, methods may appear in the target and condition parts of a query. The object management subsystem translates such methods into manipulation and predicate functions of selection or join operators, which can access tuples on page buffers and can avoid unnecessary data transfer between page buffers and application programs.

The object expressions, or implicit joins, generate several equi-joins of relations in general, which must be efficiently processed. The object management subsystem uses hash join or TID join to process such joins. If there is no index available on the OID field of joined relations, they are joined by using hash join. The order of more than one joins is dynamically determined. If there is a B-tree index available, such relations are joined by using the B-tree index. A selection predicate, if any, is evaluated during the join operation. In this case, more than one joins are processed from left to right in the object expression.

A nonleaf class in a class hierarchy is specified in a query. In the case of selection of a nonleaf class, the query is expanded into queries against the leaf subclasses. In the case of join with a nonleaf class, the intermediate results of selection or join operators before the nonleaf class join are switched to separate relations, each of which includes only OIDs of a single leaf class as a join key. Then relevant relations are joined, which can avoid unnecessary search.

Multiple-valued attributes are usually unnested before processing. If aggregate functions or universally-quantified conditions are applied to multiple-valued attributes together with prohibition of unnesting, they undergo no automatic unnesting of attribute values.

Semantic query optimization uses semantic information such as categorization. If a condition on the categorization attribute specified by a query matches some of the categorization conditions of partition subclasses, the query is specialized into the query against the matched subclasses.

(4) Object buffering

The object management subsystem provides object buffers for efficient object access from programs, in addition to page buffers provided by the data management subsystem. Object buffers are basically a hash table for in-memory object management. An object referenced through its OID is hashed by the OID as a key to make a hash entry and an in-memory instance data structure. The hash entry contains the pointer to the instance data structure, the OID, the TID, the status flags, and the next pointer.

If objects are referenced by other objects resident in object buffers, the OID-to-pointer mapping is done by the hash table and the pointer to the instance data structure is cashed to the attributes of the referencing objects. At later access, the object can be directly accessed by the pointer without hashing. If an object is newly created or updated, the status flag of the hash entry is set to create or update. When a transaction is committed, they are flushed to page buffers. If objects resident in object buffers are swapped out for memory management, the status is set to free. When the object is accessed again, the instance data structure is created by directly fetching the object from databases through the TID of the hash entry for the object.

If an object is destroyed, the status flag is set to destroy. If the object is accessed later, reference validity is checked for referential integrity. Introducing object buffers in addition to page buffers makes different versions of the same objects. To evaluate a query, the object management subsystem flushes the newly created or updated objects from the object buffers to the page buffers and evaluates the query against the page buffers. The combinational use of object buffers and page buffers can support the integration of programming and query facilities at an architecture level.

4.1 System Architecture

Jasmine has a layered architecture consisting of the data management subsystem and the object management subsystem (See Figure 4.1). The data management subsystem is an extended relational DBMS which provides operation interfaces for nested relations, tuples, and pages. It is an extensible database system [CARE88] as described later. In contrast, the object management subsystem provides an object model, language compiler and run-time support library, and language interpreter. Our approach is to provide an object-oriented model and language interface to an extensible database system, such as GENESIS [BATO88] and EXODUS [CARE88].

This layered approach has advantages. First, the approach makes the system flexible in the following way. No definite way to implement an object-oriented DBMS is yet known. The implemented system is subject to further refinement. The whole system needs flexibility as a test bed. If the system is constructed as a monolithic system or collection of specialized subsystems, it would be less flexible to such refinement.

Persistent objects are efficiently stored and accessed by the data management subsystem. In general, operations of objects are compiled into those of the data management subsystem and are executed efficiently with run-time support. Optimization is done at compilation.

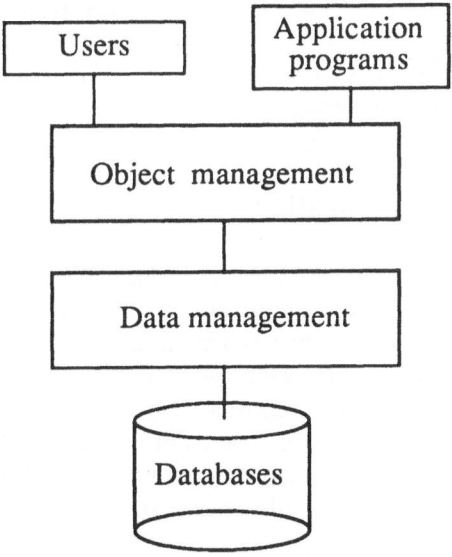

Figure 4.1. System architecture.

4.2 Data Management Subsystem

The data management subsystem, an general-purpose extended relational database kernel, provides nested relations and their operations so that it can efficiently store objects, which have hierarchical structures such as attribute, facet, and value. Note that a theoretical basis for the nested relational model was provided by Kitagawa and Kunii [KITA89]. It provides three access methods for relations to efficiently access objects stored in relations. The user of this subsystem can choose among sequential, B-tree, and hash relations. Indexes of sequential relations are implemented by using B-tree relations.

Inner relations for nested relations can be supported by all of the access methods. This subsystem provides a variety of methods, such as nested loop, hash join, and tuple substitution, to efficiently process equijoins generated by most set-oriented queries of objects.

The data management subsystem aims to have as few limitations as possible. The maximum number of fields is unlimited. The page size is variable for each relation to contain multimedia data such as images within one page and to make it recoverable. This subsystem supports only two data types, fixed-length field and variable-length field, so that the subsystem is transparent about data types and is able to assimilate any new data types without being changed. The subsystem has no built-in optimizer so that the user of the subsystem can control optimization explicitly. New applications need a variety of operations to filter and manipulate data. The operations are compiled into manipulation and predicate functions which can process tuples on a buffer directly. The data management subsystem can be viewed as a naked extensible DBMS. This subsystem is used by the object management subsystem to implement the object model and the object manipulation language.

4.2.1   Relation organization

(1) Sequential relations are the most basic relations. The data management subsystem provides two data types, fixed-length and variable-length fields. The tuple has the structure depicted in Figure 4.2. The fore part of the tuple contains the fixed-length data and the offset data of the variable-length data. The variable-length data together with its length is stored in the latter part of the tuple. This scheme allows any data in a tuple to be accessed in a constant time. Modification of the variable-length data can be done without affecting the fixed-length data. Any field or group of fields can be indexed. The user of the subsystem can specify null values as special values.

(2) Hash relations consist of key fields and nonkey fields. The hash function is supplied by the user. Hash relations are based on one of the dynamic hashing schemes called *linear hashing with partial expansion* [LARS80], whose merits include space expansion proportional to data quantity and adjustable, high ratio of space utilization.

(3) B-tree relations also consist of key fields and nonkey fields. Comparison of key data at insertion and range check at search are done by the user-supplied functions. This allows new access methods, such as R-tree [GUTT84], to be assimilated by supplying dedicated comparison and range functions. B-tree relations used as an index on sequential relations consist of several key fields and one TID field. This corresponds to a *non-clustered index*. B-tree relations which contain the whole data can be viewed as relations with a *clustered index*.

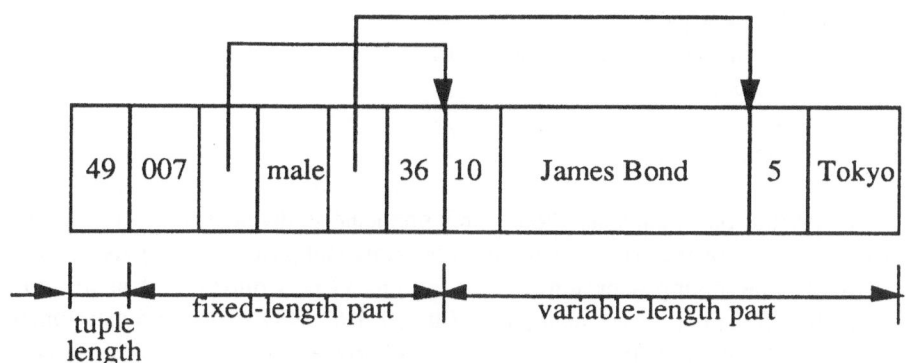

Figure 4.2. Tuple structure.

(4)Inner relations of nested relations are assumed to be rather small, so we implement inner relations by sequentially storing them in variable-length fields of relations to improve locality of access. In particular, hash and B-tree based relations can contain inner relations only in their nonkey fields. So nested relations can allow sequential, hash, and B-tree based access for atomic fields or key fields but allow only sequential access for inner relations or nonkey fields. We provide nest and unnest operations for nested relations in addition to retrieval, insertion, deletion, and update. Retrieved inner relations can be operated as sequential relations. Update of inner relations can be done by retrieving inner relations, updating them as sequential relations and replacing old ones by new ones. We provide the functions interpreting the variable-length fields according the nested relation schemes to operate on inner relations.

4.2.2 Predicate and manipulation functions

Some applications need to filter data by complex procedures which cannot be represented by a combination of simple conditions and other applications need to manipulate it. Conventionally, the applications themselves have to retrieve all data and filter and manipulate it. This approach is inefficient because extra data transfer and conversion between buffer and application programs is required. In addition, system-defined general-purpose comparators which interpret any data according to data types are inefficient.

A *predicate function* and *manipulation function* are used to solve these problems. Predicate functions are defined by the user to filter data. For example, the following predicate function filters tuples by using the program *critical*:

```
predicate1 (flag, OID, condition, room, age)
  { if (flag == MAIN)
    { if ( critical() == true && age > 50)
        return true
      else
        return false } }
```

The variable flag indicates whether this predicate is invoked for PREprocessing, MAINprocessing, or POSTprocessing. Preprocessing and postprocessing are done only once while the mainprocessing is done tuple-wise. Control is transferred to manipulation functions which manipulate filtered data only if the predicate function returns true. The predicate functions are compiled into operations on tuples in buffer

and are efficiently processed because no type is dynamically checked and no data is interpreted. A simple condition with the system-defined comparison operators such as == is also defined as a predicate function which is compiled like the user-defined complex condition:

```
predicate2 (flag, OID, name)
  { if (flag == MAIN)
    { if (name == "James Bond")
        return true
      else
        return false } }
```

If no predicate is explicitly supplied, control is always passed to manipulation functions.

Manipulation functions supplied by the user are invoked only if predicate functions return true. They are compiled to operate directly on tuples in the buffer. For example, the following manipulation function operates on tuples of a relation by using a make-medical-certificate program and inserts the result into another relation tmp3:

```
manipulate3 (flag, OID, doctor, name, disease)
  { if (flag == PRE)
      openinsert(tmp3);
    else if (flag == MAIN)
    { result = make-medical-certificate("19890214");
      insert(tmp3, result);}
    else if (flag == POST)
      closeinsert(tmp3);}
```

Simple retrieval of fields, projection, is defined as a manipulation function which returns the fields. For example, the following manipulation function inserts a field OID of a relation into another relation tmp1:

```
manipulate4(flag, OID)
{ if (flag == PRE)
    openinsert(tmp1);
  else if (flag == MAIN)
    insert(tmp1, OID);
  else if (flag == POST)
    closeinsert(tmp1);}
```

In general, selection and join operators described below require predicate and manipulation functions. Data is thus efficiently filtered by predicate functions and manipulated by manipulation functions.

4.2.3 Operators

The data management subsystem provides relational operators as functions. **select** is a selection operator. **hjoin** performs hash joins [YAMA85], its hash function being supplied by the user. **tjoin** joins tuples based on TID. **join** does nested loops. **sort** sorts data by combining quicksort and multi-way mergesort. The comparison function is supplied by the user. **unique** eliminates duplicates of data based on hashing. **nest** and **unnest** are used for conversion between flat and nested relations. Update operators such as **insert, delete**, and **update**, are also supported.

These relational operators are programmed using the tuple operators such as scan, raster, access, fetch, delete, and update. These tuple operators have the same interfaces for all types of relations. The relational layer can be programmed by the general tuple operators without distinguishing between relation types. So even if new type relations are added to the tuple layer, the relational layer needs almost no modification. This is, so to speak, an object-oriented implementation of a relational database system.

4.2.4 Implementation detail

We discuss the implementation of data management for advanced applications in detail.

(1) Data structures

In conventional relational database systems, data dictionaries and indexes are provided as system functions. Such functions are usually implemented not as relations but as special data structures because of access efficiency. This prevents the user from customizing them. Some indexes may be maintained with the deferred-update strategy and others with the immediate-update strategy. Some applications may require both clustered and non-clustered indexes and others may require both hash and B-tree indexes. Application-specific information may be added to data dictionaries. Therefore, the data management subsystem supports only relations (sequential, B-tree, hash, and inner relations), and allows the user of this subsystem to implement customized data dictionaries and indexes by using relations.

The data management subsystem only supports fixed-length and variable-length data as field types of tuples. The data management subsystem makes no interpretation of field values except for TIDs and inner relations. Any type of data can be stored such as an array, a list, and a relation. Inner relations can be implemented as variable-length fields. Inner relations can have other inner relations as field values, so nested relations can be recursively defined. The length of a tuple must be less than the page size for efficient access and simple implementation. The length and number of fields in a tuple are subject to this limit. Note that the page size can change from 4KB to 256KB to allow long data such as multimedia data and nested relations.

The data management subsystem supports four types of relations, as follows:

1)Sequential relation
The pages of this type of relation are sequentially linked. Tuples are stored in the order of insertion. The location of inserted tuples is fixed, so an index can be created on sequential relations.

2) B-tree relation
This type of relation has B-tree structures. Tuples are stored in the leaf pages in the order specified by user-defined order functions.

3) Hash relation
Hash relations use a dynamic hashing scheme called linear hashing with partial expansion [LARS80], an extension to linear hashing. We choose this scheme because the space required to store data is proportional to the amount of data and the space utilization ratio is adjustable and high.

4) Inner relation
Inner relations for realizing nested relations are stored in variable-length fields of tuples. Tuples of inner relations are sequentially inserted. Nested relations can be recursively implemented by storing inner relations in fields of another inner relation.

TIDs can be stored in fixed-length fields. TIDs act as pointers to tuples. A variety of data structures can be implemented by using TIDs. For example, a non-clustered index can be implemented by defining an index key field and a TID field in B-tree or hash relations (See Figure 4.3). Precomputed joins can be implemented by storing TIDs of one of the relations for joins in the field of the other relation (See Figure 4.4).

All four types of relations have the same tuple structures. The first two bytes of a tuple contain the tuple length. The tuple consists of fixed and variable parts. Fixed-length fields are stored in the fixed part. Variable-length fields are stored in the variable part. The offsets of the variable-length fields from the top of the tuple are stored in the fixed part. Any data can be accessed in a constant time although this tuple structure does not allow null-value compression.

Access to fields is a frequent operation, so it must be efficiently processed. We provide pointer arrays for field access (See Figure 4.5). Each pointer points to the corresponding field in a tuple on page buffers. Simple tuple structures allow efficient construction of pointer arrays. One alternative is to copy field values to different areas. The alternative is good for data protection, but is rather time-consuming. Field pointer arrays are passed to user-defined functions such as manipulation and predicate functions for field access.

For efficient data access, it is important to move as few data as possible and to fix tuples in buffers if possible. Internal sorting uses pointer arrays for tuples to be sorted (See Figure 4.6). Such pointers are moved instead of tuples. Similarly, when a hash table is created for internal hashing, pointers to tuples are linked instead of tuples.

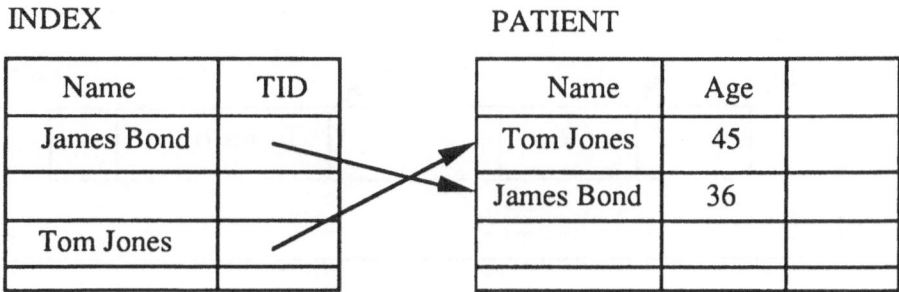

Figure 4.3. Non-clustered index using a B-tree relation.

PATIENT   DOCTOR

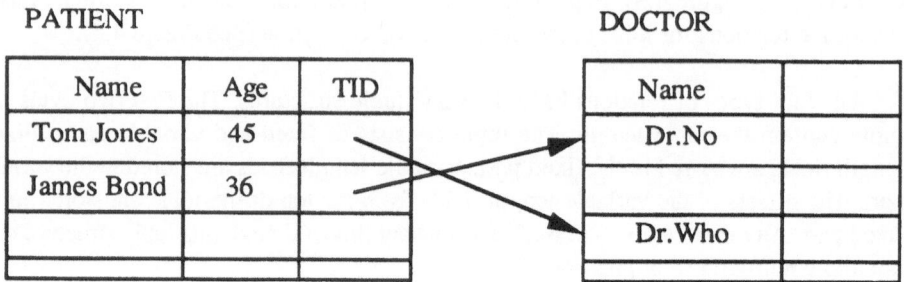

Figure 4.4. Precomputed join.

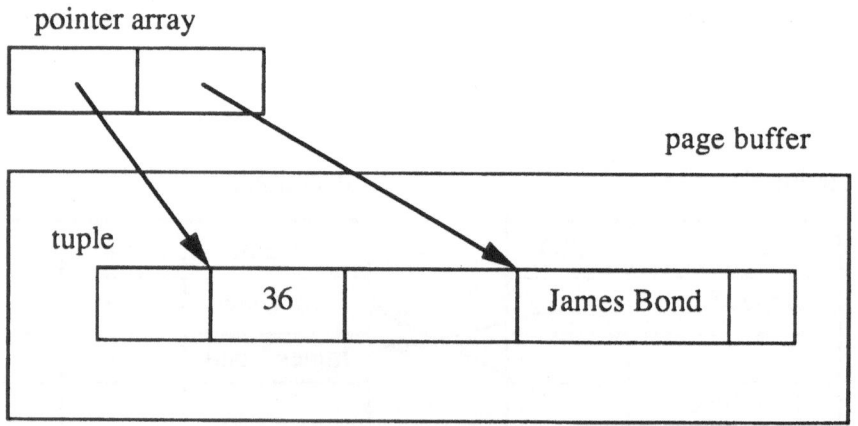

Figure 4.5. Pointer array for field access.

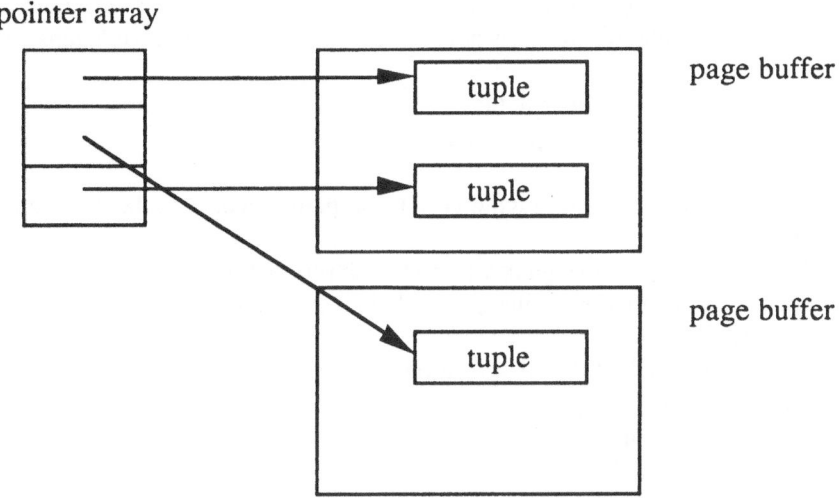

Figure. 4.6. Pointer array for internal sorting.

(2) Hash-based processing

In conventional relational databases, sorting is used to implement relational operators such as equi-join, set-difference, duplicate elimination. In equi-join, sort-based methods require O (m log m + n log n) processing time, where m and n are the number of tuples of two joined relations. If we use the hash join method, when either of two joined relations can be loaded into main memory, the processing time is O (m+n). Now that the cost of main memory is becoming lower and larger amounts of main memory are available, it will be easier to load the smaller relation of two joined relations into main memory and most of the join operations will be more efficiently processed. Even if neither of them can be loaded into main memory, the hash join method generally requires less CPU time and I/O times than the sort-based method. We adopted the hash-based method for equi-joins and other operations such as set-difference [YAMA85]. Unlike Jasmine, other object-oriented database systems such as ORION use nested-loop and sort-merge joins.

First, we describe the internal hash join algorithm, which is used when either of two input relations for joins can be loaded into main memory. Recursion is not used in the internal hash join. Only one relation is partitioned into subrelations. The other relation is only scanned tuple by tuple. It is not necessary to load both of the relations entirely.

We describe the outline of the algorithm. Only main memory is used during processing. Secondary memory is not used as a workspace.

1) Determine which input relation is to be partitioned. Let the partitioned input relation be A.

2) Determine a partition number p and a hash function h.

3) Partition the relation A into p subrelations Ai = { a belongs to A | h (key of a) = i } (0<= i <p).

4) For each tuple b of the other relation B, compute k=h(key of b) and compare each tuple of Ak with b on the join key. When they match, make a new tuple from them and output it to the output relation C. The algorithm, written in a Pascal-like language, is shown below.

```
procedure INTERNAL (A,B,C);
begin
        determine which input relation is partitioned (let it be A);
        determine a partition number p and a hash function h;
        for i:=0 to p-1 do Ai := { };
        for i:=1 to m do begin
                get a tuple ai from A;
                k := h(key of ai);
                Ak := Ak union {ai};
        end;
        for j:=1 to n do begin
                get a tuple bj from b;
                k:=h(key of bj);
                for each a belonging to Ak do
                        if key of a = key of bj
                                then generate the resulting tuple and output it to C;
        end;
end;
```

where m and n are the number of tuples of input relations A and B. We select h(x) = mod(x,p) as a hash function and p=ceiling(square-root(m*n)) as a partition number, where mod(x,y) returns the remainder of x divided by y and ceiling(x) returns the least integer greater than or equal to x.

Next we will describe the external hash join, which is used when neither of two input relations can be loaded into main memory. The essential difference between the external hash join and the internal hash join is the use of recursiveness and the partitioning of both of the input relations. The outline of the algorithm is as follows:

1) Determine a partition number p and a hash function h.

2) Partition the relation A into p subrelations A_i = { a belongs to A | h (key of a) = i} (0<= i <p), and partition B into p subrelations B_i = { b belongs to B | h (key of b) = i} (0<= i <p). Each subrelation is stored in secondary memory.

3) For each i (0<= i<p), if either A_i or B_i can be entirely loaded into main memory, A_i and B_i are joined using the internal hash join. Otherwise, steps 1) through 3) are executed recursively.

We assume that there are Z+2 buffers BUF(0), BUF(1), ... , BUF(Z+1) in main memory and that the partition number p is less than or equal to Z. BUF(Z+1) is always used for storing the resulting tuples into the output relation. The relation A is partitioned into p subrelations as follows. BUF(Z) is used to read the relation A and p buffers BUF(0), ... , BUF(p-1) of Z buffers are used to output tuples for subrelations A0, ... , Ap-1. These Z buffers are called partition buffers. The relation A is read page by page into BUF(Z), and for each tuple a in the buffer, we compute k=h(key of a) (0<=k<p) and put a in BUF(k). The content of BUF(i) (0<=i<p) is written to secondary memory when BUF(i) becomes full or when the partitioning of A is complete. The relation B is partitioned in the same way. For the internal hash join, we use Z buffers BUF(0), BUF(1), ... , BUF(Z-1) to load one subrelation and a buffer BUF(Z) to read the other subrelation. We show the external hash join algorithm below.

```
procedure EXTERNAL(A,B,C);
begin
        if either A or B is loaded into main memory
                (that is, either A or B has Z or less pages)
        then INTERNAL(A,B,C);
        else begin
                determine a hash function h and a partition number p;
                partition A into p subrelations Ai = { a belongs to A | h (key of a) = i }
                        (0<= i <p) and
                partition B into p subrelations Bi = { b belongs to B | h (key of b) = i }
                        (0<= i <p) using secondary memory;
                for i:=0 to p-1 do EXTERNAL(Ai,Bi,C);
        end;
end;
```

Objects are often referenced by the OIDs, so we provide hash relations to allow the user to directly access objects through OIDs as a hash key. We use linear hashing with partial expansion [LARS80] as a dynamic hashing scheme for hash relations. The outline of the algorithm is as follows. First, we divide a file into g groups of s buckets each. Next we need two hash functions, in (key) and hk (key), to determine the group and the bucket in the group to which a tuple belongs. Bucket expansion is done by moving parts of tuples in g buckets to g+1 buckets. By repeating this process s times, the file size increases by one group, which establishes a partial expansion. After that, bucket expansion divides g+1 buckets to g+2 buckets. By repeating g partial expansions, we get a full expansion, which doubles the file size. At this time we revert the file to g groups consisting of 2s buckets each. If we assume that the file consists of n groups of s ($=2^k$) buckets each, we take hk(key)=mod(key,2^k) and in(key) =mod(floor(key/2^k), n), where floor(x) returns the greatest integer less than or equal to x. This scheme has the advantages of space expansion proportional to data quantity and an adjustable, high ratio of space utilization.

(3) User-defined functions

Application-specific parts of application programs vary from one application to another. It is often difficult, or almost impossible, to decide which ones are to be included by the data management subsystem. The strategy to make this layer as general as possible is to separate application-specific parts, implement them as functions, and embed them into the subsystem. For implementation efficiency, the application-specific parts are implemented as user-functions which are called by the subsystem.

We describe user-defined functions given to the data management subsystem to clarify the application-specific parts of the subsystem.

1) A *predicate function* specifies a retrieval condition of selection or join operators.

2) A *manipulation function* specifies operators performed on each tuple satisfying the predicate in selection or join operators.

3) An *order function* specifies the order used by sorting or B-tree relations.

4) A *range function* specifies a search condition of B-tree relations such as a<=x<b or c<x.

5) A *static hash function* is used by hash-based relational operators such as join, union, difference, and intersection.

6) A *dynamic hash function* is used by hash relations.

Separation of application-specific parts by providing user-defined functions allows both flexible customization by the user and efficient execution by compiling.

(4) Architecture

The data management subsystem consists of three layers: relational layer, tuple layer, and storage layer (See Figure 4.7). All of these are open to the user. The data management subsystem provides no query parser or optimizer because they are rather high-level and application-dependent. The data management subsystem is just an executer of operators provided by the three layers.

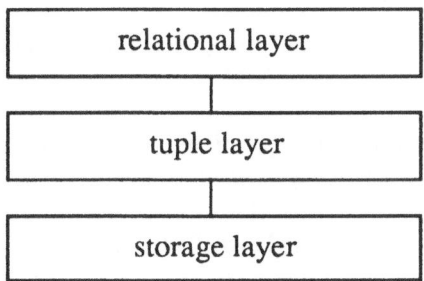

Figure 4.7. Architecture.

The relational layer provides functions which execute set operations as an extension to relational algebra. The users of the data management subsystem combine these functions to implement their needs. For example,

1) **select** (**rb**, **pb**, **mb**) extends selection of relational algebra. It has three parameters **rb**, **pb**, and **mb**. **rb** is the data block which specifies the source relation. **pb** and **mb** specify user-defined predicate and manipulation functions, respectively.

2) **hjoin(rb1, rb2, mb, hb)** performs equi-join of relations specifying **rb1** and **rb2**. **mb** is performed on each pair of tuples which match on join fields. This operation is based on a hash function specified by **hb**.

3) **join(rb1, rb2, pb, mb)** performs a general join of relations **rb1** and **rb2**.

4) **tjoin(rb1, rb2, tid, mb)** joins each tuple of **rb1** with a tuple of **rb2** pointed by its **tid** field and performs **mb** on such a pair of tuples.

5) **sort(rb1, rb2, ob)** sorts **rb1** and stores the result into **rb2**. The order function is specified by **ob**.

6) **unique(rb1, rb2, hb)** eliminates duplicates of **rb1** and stores the result into

rb2. This operation is hash-based.

7) **nest(rb1, rb2, fid, hb)** generates a nested relation **rb2** from a flat relation **rb1** with fields specified by **fid**. This operation is also hash-based.

8) **unnest(rb1, rb2, fid)** generates a flat relation **rb2** from a nested relation **rb1**.

Functions of the tuple layer operate on four types of relations. The operators are as follows:

1) **scan** scans a relation sequentially and finds a tuple satisfying the specified predicate.

2) **raster** scans a relation sequentially fixing scanned pages on buffers. This operation is used in internal sorting or in making internal hash tables.

3) **access** directly accesses a tuple satisfying the specified predicate.

4) **fetch** directly accesses a tuple specified by a given TID.

5) **insert** inserts a tuple or a group of fields.

6) **delete** deletes a tuple specified by a given TID.

7) **update** updates a tuple specified by a given TID.

8) **clear** deletes all tuples.

9) **flac** constructs a field pointer array for the specified fields.

This layer conceals the physical structures of tuples or relations. The operator interfaces are similar for all four types of relations, so the relational layer can be almost independent of the relation types. When a new type of relation is added, the relational layer is not so much affected, as long as the interface similarity is kept.

The storage layer provides disk I/O, page buffers, transactions, concurrency control, and recovery. Disk I/O management includes allocation and deallocation of subdatabases (segments) and pages. A database consists of two types of subdatabases. One is a subdatabase which is permanent and recoverable. The other is a subdatabase which is used as a workspace for keeping temporary relations, and is only effective in a transaction. This is not recoverable. Subdatabases are composed of a number of pages.

The storage layer supports variable-length pages. A variable-length page consists of several 4KB physical pages, which form a virtually continuous page on buffers. Its length can vary: 2^iKB (i=2, 3, 4, 5, 6, 7, 8). We use the buddy system for buffer space allocation. The page length can be specified for each relation because multimedia data and inner relations may exceed 4KB.

Concurrency control is based on granularity, two-phase locking. Deadlock detection is done by examining a cycle in the Wait-For-Graph. One of the deadlocked transactions in the cycle in the graph is chosen as the victim for rollback. ORION uses deadlock detection based on the use of timeouts. Our transaction recovery is based on shadow-paging for simplicity.

4.3   Object Management Subsystem

We will describe how we implemented the object management subsystem by using the data management subsystem. First, we will explain how to store objects. Then, after describing the language compiler and run-time support focusing on query optimization and object buffering, we will explain the interpreter.

4.3.1   Storage structures of objects

We will discuss storage of instance objects and class objects by use of the data management subsystem. Storage structures differ from instance to class. Translation of objects to relations is automatically done by the system. Information about the translation is held by classes.

PATIENT

Oid	Sex	Age	Name	Doctor	Category	Temperature	Weight	Height	
MedicalPatient007	male	36	James Bond	MedicalDoctor000	inpatient	36.5 37.3 38.1	76.0	181.0	

Figure 4.8. Example of an instance table.

(1) Instance storage by use of relations.

All intrinsic instances of a REFERENCE class are stored in a relation, corresponding an instance to a tuple and an attribute to a field (See Figure 4.8). Multiple-valued attributes such as Temperature are stored as a multiple-valued field, the simplest form of nested relations. Alternatively, implementing multiple-valued attributes by separate relations would cause extra joins. We treat inherited attributes such as Age and newly-defined attributes such as Weight uniformly. This is called *horizontal splitting*, and is more efficient than alternatives such as *vertical splitting* and *triples* [NIXO87]. We store intrinsic instances of a superclass and those of a subclass in separate relations. If we instantiate or destroy intrinsic instances of a class, we don't have to propagate any modification to its superclass or subclass. This allows us to modify objects efficiently.

Fixed-length strings and numbers are stored in fixed-length fields and variable-length strings are stored in variable-length fields. As for reference attributes such as Doctor we store only OIDs in fixed-length fields. This implements non-clustered complex objects. Non-clustered complex objects are needed by CAD applications where complex objects are created bottom-up, that is, component objects are reused. Of course, the user may enforce complex object integrity on non-clustered complex objects logically. This can be done by attaching an *after* demon instantiating component objects to the instantiate method of whole objects and by attaching a *before* demon destroying component objects to the destroy method of whole objects [ISHI90]. As for relation objects in attributes, we make full use of nested relations. We correspond relation objects to inner relations of nested relations and their attributes to fields of the inner relations. Inherently, component objects of relation objects cannot exist without their whole objects. Clustered complex objects, implemented by relation objects, can be managed as a unit both logically and physically.

The Oid attribute corresponds to a field, but the Class attribute and common attributes such as Cardinality are not stored in instance relations. This is for increased space efficiency. An OID consists of a database id-number, a class id-number, and an instance id-number, so an OID alone can inform us of its database and class information directly. According to the user specification, the system chooses among sequential, B-tree, and hash relations as instance storage. The user can attach indexes to attributes of sequential relation-based objects. B-tree and hash relations always require key attributes.

(2) Class storage by use of relations.

As classes are instances of CLASS, we store all classes in one relation and facilitate efficient associative access of class objects. Classes, however, have heterogeneous structures, so we have to devise a scheme which contains them in one relation efficiently. Basically we correspond one class object to one tuple. Since attribute categorization, such as enumerated and procedural, is common to all classes and attributes have a fixed set of facets, we store enumerated and procedural attributes in different inner relations and facets in the fields of the inner relations. The system-defined attributes such as Super are stored in separate fields (See Figure 4.9). This scheme is naturally derived by the definition of CLASS which uses relation objects to avoid joins of sequential relations. This can store heterogeneous classes in one relation and make set-oriented access efficient. Alternatively, to correspond each attribute to a separate field would make the scheme inflexibly large and would generate too much null data.

CLASS

Name	Db	Super	Property							
			name	class	mandatory	multiple	constraint	if-needed		
PATIENT	MEDICAL	PERSON	Doctor	DOCTOR	yes					
			Category	STRING						
			Temperature	FLOAT		yes	Cons020			
			Weight	FLOAT	yes		Cons021			
			Height	FLOAT			Cons022	Demon030		

CLASS (continued)

	Method					
	name	class	multiple	main	before	after
	make-medical-certificate	MEDICAL_CERTIFICATE		Metod001		

Figure 4.9. Example of a class table.

4.3.2 Set-oriented access support

Both set-oriented access and singleton access are compiled to do early binding and reduce run-time overhead. However, an interactive query needed by application development is processed by the interpreter, not by the compiler. The Jasmine compiler is implemented using a C compiler. The application programs written in Jasmine/C are precompiled to C programs and the generated C programs are compiled and linked with the run-time support library. Preprocessing is used to take maximum advantage of portability and code optimization of the C compiler (See Figure 4.10). The interpreter executes a string of Jasmine/C directly (See Figure 4.11). In this and the following subsections we describe support for set-oriented and singleton access, focusing on the compiler.

Application programs are translated into C in three phases: *query graph generation*, *access plan generation*, and *code generation*. The first phase generates a query graph from the user query and transforms the query graph to a more efficient one by using the object model defined by the user. The second phase generates an optimal plan of a series of relational operators according to the query graph. This phase uses a rule-based optimization technique. Lastly, the C codes are generated to feed the C compiler.

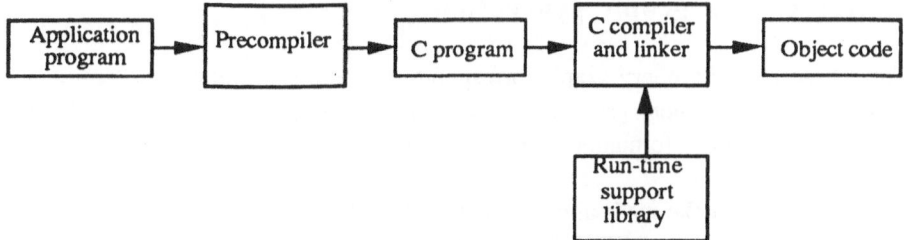

(a) compiling

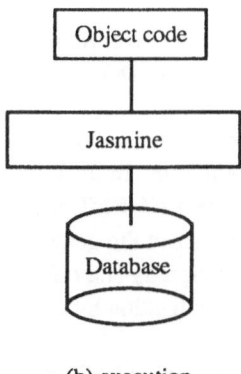

(b) execution

Figure 4.10. Complier.

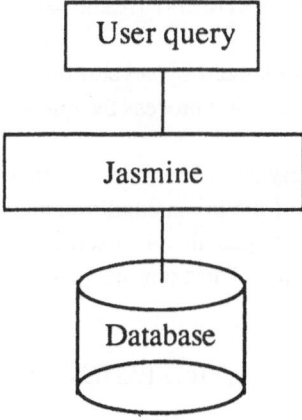

Figure 4.11. Interpreter.

4.3.2.1 Query graph generation

This phase makes a query graph corresponding to the user query by referencing the object model. The query graph is a subgraph of the object model annotated with the target and condition information. For example, consider the query:

> PATIENT.make-medical-certificate("19890214")
>   where PATIENT.critical() == true
>   and PATIENT.Age > 50
>   and PATIENT.Doctor.Name == "Dr. No"

This makes the following query graph:

> ADULT-PATIENT (make-medical-certificate("19890214"), critical() == true,
>   Age > 50, DOCTOR (Name == " Dr. No"))

During this phase, the user query containing incomplete knowledge access is transformed into a more efficient one. In Jasmine, the user can form a query by specifying a general class such as PATIENT instead of the specific class ADULT-PATIENT. Then it is necessary to restrict the general class to its appropriate subclass in order to process the original query correctly and efficiently. The techniques needed include specialization by attributes and specialization by categorization conditions.

We describe the specialization techniques. First, the user can form a query specifying a class followed by an attribute which is defined in its subclass. Specialization of the class by the attribute is required to process this correctly and efficiently. For example, the example query (11) of Section 3.1.3 generates the following query graph:

> DOCTOR (Name, DEPARTMENT (Name == "surgery"))

If different classes are specialized by several object expressions, the most specific class is chosen to restrict the class and process the query efficiently.

Second, the user can specify a nonleaf class together with conditions concerning the categorization attribute. Then if the given condition matches some of the categorization conditions, the nonleaf class is specialized to some of the partition members with the matched categorization condition. The example query (12) of Section 3.1.3 is translated as follows:

> CHILD (OID, Age < 13) CHILD-PATIENT (OID, Age < 13)

In general, the query against a nonleaf class can generate multiple subclass queries like this. However, the query of intrinsic instances by the attribute Class is restricted to the nonleaf class itself. For example, the example query (13) of Section 3.1.3 generates the query graph:

PERSON (Name, Address == "Tokyo")

This denotes retrieval of intrinsic instances of PERSON only.

4.3.2.2 Access plan generation

This phase translates the query graph into object operators in a pattern-directed fashion. The translation rules are constructed based on query semantics using object operators described previously. Then object operators are transformed into extended relational operators using the object model information such as statistics, access methods, and mapping from class to relation. The object expression is processed differently depending on whether it contains a procedural attribute.

First consider the case where the object expression has no procedural attributes. In general, the object expression in the target or condition part generates equijoins between instance relations corresponding to a functional join. In addition, the conditions generate selections and explicit joins. For equijoin, a predicate function which joins two instance relations by an attribute field of one relation and an OID field of the other is generated. For selection, a condition concerning one instance relation is generated as a predicate function of a select operator. It can include a logical combination of simple conditions. For an explicit join, a join predicate function which may contain non-equijoin is generated. Manipulation functions are generated to project fields for later operation.

Inherited and newly-defined attributes are processed in the same way because both of them are stored in the same relation. If a multiple-valued attribute is specified in an object expression, the result of the relational operator, selection or join, is automatically unnested unless its prohibition is specified. The query results in a set of OIDs, values, or tuples. A query against a nonleaf class evaluates to a relation containing OIDs of instances of several classes. As OIDs have the same structure for all objects, they can be stored in one relation. Each object scan returns an object, by scanning the result relation and then selecting the base instance relation by the OID (tuple substitution). At that time, if an object is already on core, it is used.

Basically, if a selection predicate of the sequential relation can use an index, selection by index is chosen which selects a B-tree relation for the index by the key condition, and sorts the result relation containing TIDs and then joins the result relation and the original sequential relation by using TIDs. The rest of the selection condition is evaluated at the same time. For B-tree and hash relations, if a predicate concerns the key fields, key-based searching is done. Notice that if a whole relation of any type is small enough to be contained within one page, sequential access is chosen.

If one of two relations being joined is contained within a page and the join key is indexed by the other relation, the *tuple substitution* is chosen. If one of two relations is contained within a page and no index is provided, the *nested loop* is chosen. Otherwise, hash join is chosen. For B-tree and hash relations, the join is similarly processed. Selection operators are done before join operators. In case of a join of several relations, the order of join is dynamically determined by the size of the intermediate result relations.

Next, we describe how to translate object expressions containing procedural attributes. User procedural attributes appearing in the target part are translated into manipulation functions. Procedural attributes in conditions are translated into predicate functions. For example, the top query of Section 4.3.2.1

> PATIENT.make-medical-certificate("19890214")
>   where PATIENT.critical() == true
>   and PATIENT.Age > 50
>   and PATIENT.Doctor.Name == "Dr. No"

is translated into a query graph and into object operators as follows:

query graph

> ADULT-PATIENT (make-medical-certificate ("19890214"),
>   critical() == true,
>   Age > 50,DOCTOR(Name == "Dr.No"))

object operators

> project(join(restrict-apply(ADULT-PATIENT, Acertificate,
>   make-medical-certificate, critical, Age > 50),
>   restrict(DOCTOR, Name=="Dr.No"), Doctor==Oid), <Acertificate>)

Then these object operators generate the relational operator sequence and the predicate and manipulation functions as follows:

```
select(DOCTOR, predicate1, manipulate1);
select(ADULT-PATIENT, predicate2, manipulate2);
if (within-page(tmp1) || within-page(tmp2))
  join(tmp1, tmp2, predicate3, manipulate3);
else
  hjoin(tmp1, tmp2, predicate3, manipulate3, hashfunc);


predicate1 (flag, OID, name)
  { if (flag == MAIN)
    { if (name == "Dr. No")
        return true
      else
        return false }}

manipulate1(flag, OID)
  { if (flag == PRE)
      openinsert(tmp1);
    else if (flag == MAIN)
      insert(tmp1, OID);
    else if (flag == POST)
      closeinsert(tmp1);}

predicate2 (flag, OID, condition, room, age)
  { if (flag == MAIN)
    { if ( critical() == true && age > 50)
        return true
      else
        return false }}

manipulate2 (flag, OID, doctor, name, disease)
  { if (flag == PRE)
      openinsert(tmp2);
    else if (flag == MAIN)
      {Acertificate = make-medical-certificate("19890214");
      insert(tmp2, doctor, Acertificate); }
    else if (flag == POST)
      closeinsert(tmp2);}
```

```
predicate3 (flag, OID, doctor)
  { if (flag == MAIN)
    { if (OID == doctor)
       return true
     else
       return false } }

manipulate3 (flag, Acertificate)
  { if (flag == PRE)
     openinsert(tmp3);
   else if (flag == MAIN)
     insert(tmp3, Acertificate);
   else if (flag == POST)
     closeinsert(tmp3);}
```

Note that the first select will be replaced by the sequence select-sort-tjoin (*selection by index*) if we assume an index on Name of DOCTOR. The system-defined procedural attributes such as aggregate functions and update functions are also translated into manipulation functions. In particular, the update functions are translated into relational update operators. As the predicate and manipulation functions directly operate on data in a buffer, they can be efficiently processed. If demons are defined and the option is specified, they are integrated into manipulation and predicate functions. The update functions generate if-added, if-removed, and if-updated demons. The reference of the object expression generates if-needed demons. If no option is specified, no code is generated.

4.3.2.3 Object-oriented query optimization

Query optimization in an object-oriented database has features different from those of query optimization in a relational database because, multiple-valued attributes, implicit joins, procedural attributes (methods), and nonleaf classes in a class hierarchy are specified in a query. First, we describe processing of multiple-valued attributes. As for non-clustered complex objects, reference attributes contain only OIDs and multiple-valued attributes contain only elements of a set. Then multiple-valued attributes contain a set of OIDs or values. Since only sequential access is supported for inner relations of nested relations, multiple-valued attributes are unnested into flat relations and are optimized conventionally, except for the application of aggregate functions. As for clustered complex objects implemented by relation objects, predicate and manipulation functions of inner relations of nested relations are nested into those of outer relations of the nested relations. They are recursively evaluated from outer relations to inner relations.

We describe implicit joins of relations generated by object expressions such as DOCTOR.Patient.Age. If there is no available index on the OID field of the relation for the class of the attribute (e.g., PATIENT), the join is processed by hash joins. The order of more than one joins is dynamically determined by the size of the intermediate result relations. If there is an index available on the OID, the join is processed by TID joins. Section predicates, if any, are evaluated during join processing. In case of several joins, they are processed from left to right in the object expression. There are methods for precomputing joins. For example, to process the query (DOCTOR.Patient.Age where DOCTOR.Patient.Age > 30), an index with Age as a key value and the OID of DOCTOR as a pointer value is created. However, it is rather difficult to maintain such an index properly.

Processing of queries containing nonleaf classes in a class hierarchy is described. We assume that PATIENT has ADULT-PATIENT and CHILD-PATIENT as subclasses. Consider the following examples,

(1) PATIENT.Name where PATIENT.Age > 8
(2) DOCTOR.Patient.Name where DOCTOR.Name == "Dr.No"
(3) DEPARTMENT.Doctor.Patient.Name where DEPARTMENT.Name == "surgery"

For the query (1), the system generates two subqueries:

result = ADULT-PATIENT.Name where ADULT-PATIENT.Age > 8
result = result + CHILD-PATIENT.Name where CHILD-PATIENT.Age > 8

The two query results are inserted into the same output relation.

For the query (2), the selection on DOCTOR class is performed first. During the selection, the intermediate output relations are switched according to the class to which the object with the OID contained by the attribute Patient of DOCTOR belongs. The class can be determined just by looking at the OID. The pseudo queries go as follows:

adult-intermediate = DOCTOR.Patient where DOCTOR.Name == "Dr.No"
and DOCTOR.Patient.Class == <ADULT-PATIENT>
child-intermediate = DOCTOR.Patient where DOCTOR.Name == "Dr.No"
and DOCTOR.Patient.Class == <CHILD-PATIENT>

Of course, the switching is done within one selection operation. The check of the class is translated into the manipulation function of the selection operator. Then adult-intermediate and ADULT-PATIENT are joined into an output relation. Child-intermediate and CHILD-PATIENT are joined into the same output relation.

For the query (3), the join of DEPARTMENT and DOCTOR is processed first.

During the join processing, the intermediate output relations are switched according to the class of the OID for DEPARTMENT.Doctor.Patient. The pseudo queries go as follows:

> adult-intermediate = DEPARTMENT.Doctor.Patient
>   where DEPARTMENT.Name == "surgery"
>   and DEPARTMENT.Doctor.Patient.Class == <ADULT-PATIENT>
> child-intermediate = DEPARTMENT.Doctor.Patient
>   where DEPARTMENT.Name == "surgery"
>   and DEPARTMENT.Doctor.Patient.Class == <CHILD-PATIENT>

The switching is done during a single join operation. The code for the switching is translated into the manipulation function of the join operator. Then a pair of adult-intermediate and ADULT-PATIENT and a pair of child-intermediate and CHILD-PATIENT are joined, and the results are merged. As described above, the intermediate result of selection or join operations is switched to separate relations, which contain only OIDs relevant to successive joins. This can establish optimal preconditions for the joins by avoiding unnecessary search.

Inherited attributes such as Age are shared by classes (PERSON, DOCTOR, PATIENT) in a class hierarchy. Basically, there are two methods for creating indexes on classes in a class hierarchy. One method is to create only one index on a whole class hierarchy, called a class-hierarchy index. The other is to create a separate index, called a single-class index, on each class. Jasmine uses single-class indexes. Other systems such as ORION and O2 use class-hierarchy indexes. The class-hierarchy index has an advantage in that the total size of index pages and the total number of accessed index pages are smaller than those of the single-class index. However, it is not always optimal when a class hierarchy is partially specified in a query. Moreover, it is rather difficult to maintain such class-hierarchy indexes.

Semantic information, such as categorization, can be used to specialize nonleaf classes to specific ones. When a condition on the categorization attribute such as (Age < 7) is specified in a query containing a nonleaf class PATIENT, if the condition matches one of the categorization conditions of partition classes (Age <18 for CHILD-PATIENT), the nonleaf class (PATIENT) is specialized into the subclass (CHILD-PATIENT) with the matched categorization condition. This can limit the search space for the query.

Methods such as make-medical-certificate of PATIENT specified in a query are translated into the manipulation and predicate functions of selection or join operators, and are processed on page buffers, which avoids unnecessary data transfer between page buffers and application programs. Methods defined by a query such as intern of DEPARTMENT is expanded into the outer query.The source codes and compiled codes for methods and demons are stored as program objects in databases. They are retrieved and compiled during query optimization. To store programs in databases makes the integration of query and programming facilities more elegant than to store them in ordinary program files.

4.3.3 Singleton access support and object buffering

Like set-oriented access, singleton access is compiled into C programs, which are compiled and linked with the run-time support library. First, run-time support will be described.

The first access of an object fetches the object from secondary memory to the page buffer. Then the object is cached in the *active object table* (AOT), a dedicated internal hash table (See Figure 4.12). AOT has an OID key and an entry consisting of a pointer to internal instance structures, TID, and several flags for update. The internal structure of an instance is similar to that of a tuple, which makes reference and conversion easy. When a transaction ends, the object with update flags on is transferred from AOT to the page buffer and to secondary memory. The user can control conflict resolution in AOT by specifying the size of AOT. For space management, objects may be deleted from AOT, but OIDs and TIDs remain to fetch an object missed at later access from databases directly.

The primary function of AOT, object buffers, is the look up of objects. When an instance is referenced through its OID for the first time, the instance is hashed by its OID as a hash key. A hash entry (an object descriptor) and an in-memory instance data structure are created. The hash entry points to the instance data structure. If the instance is referenced through its OID by other instances resident in AOT, the OID is mapped to the pointer to the hash entry through the AOT hash table. And the pointer can be cashed into the attribute of the referencing instance since an OID is longer than a physical pointer. At successive access, the instance can be directly accessed by the pointer without hashing.

AOT has another important role to maintain the status flags for update of objects. When an object is newly created or updated, the status flag in the hash entry for the object is set to create or update. When a transaction is committed, the object with the status create or update is modified or added into the page buffers. When an object is destroyed, the corresponding in-memory instance data structure is deallocated and the status flag is changed to destroy. After that, if the destroyed object is referenced, the validity of reference is checked and an exception handler is invoked. This can support referential integrity. When a transaction is committed, the object is destroyed in databases.

When AOT is full of objects, extraneous objects are swapped out. Such an object is flushed to the page buffers and the in-memory instance data structure is deallocated and the status flag in the hash entry is set to free. When the object is referenced again, the object is directly fetched from databases to AOT through its TID registered in the hash entry

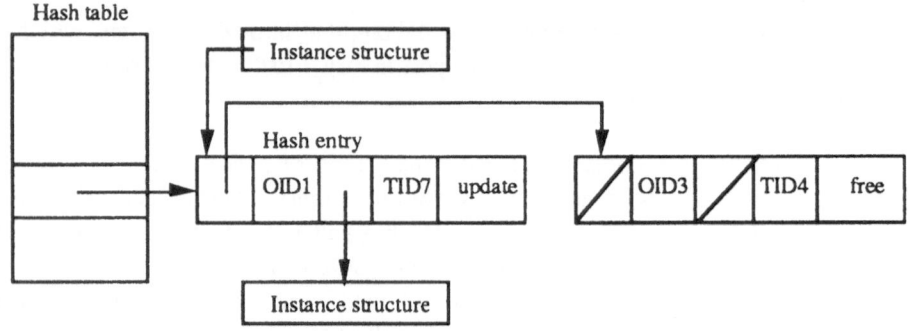

Figure 4.12. AOT structure.

We describe translation of an object expression in singleton access into AOT-based access. Consider the object expression *obj.attr* at the right-hand side of a statement. The variable *obj* holds a pointer to an AOT entry. First, the update flag of the AOT entry is checked. If the flag indicates that the object is deleted, an error occurs. If the object is cleared from main memory for space management, the object is directly fetched from secondary memory by using TID. Otherwise the system gets the *attr* field of the internal instance structure pointed to by the AOT entry. If the *attr* field has an immediate value, this object expression results in this value. If the field holds a reference object, that is, OID, the system searches an object with the OID in AOT by hashing. If absent, the object is retrieved from secondary memory by either OID or TID and cached in AOT. Then the value of the object expression evaluates to the pointer to the AOT entry corresponding to the reference object as the value of the *attr* field. The general object expression *obj.attr-1...attr-n* is recursively translated. Like this, the object variable holds a pointer to an AOT entry, not an OID at later access. Object access is thus accelerated by avoiding a hash-based search. In particular, this is important for *link-based object access* such as hypermedia applications [HALA88].

The object expression at the left-hand side of a statement is expanded similarly except that the *attr* field is updated. In case of update, the update flag is set on and the object is stored in secondary memory at the transaction end. In particular, the destroy operation of an instance sets the destroy flag and frees the areas. Basically, we only check the validity of reference, but we leave maintenance of referential integrity to the user because automatic maintenance may propagate wrong updates. Of course, the user can have automatic enforcement of referential integrity by supplying the destroy attribute with the side effect demon which deletes the destroyed object from the attribute of referencing objects.

The result of the multiple-valued attribute in singleton access is set to a set variable as described previously. Although the internal representation of the set variable in this case is a list for efficient access, but not a relation, the set variable is scanned in the same way as in set-oriented access.

Procedural attributes are replaced by invocation of the compiled functions with appropriate parameters. Polymorphism is implemented by expanding into a C switch statement with each case corresponding to a subclass attribute. Procedural attributes and demons are compiled at class definition and managed by program objects. The system-defined attributes are compiled in advance and the compiled functions are also referenced.

Now we describe why the object management subsystem requires AOT in addition to page buffers of the data management subsystem. In general, buffers are directly associated with patterns of access of objects. Page buffers have structures suitable for access of different instances of the same class. AOT, object buffers, have structures suitable for access of correlated instances of different classes. Advanced applications such as CAD have combinations of two such patterns. This necessitates a dual buffer scheme consisting of page buffers and object buffers, not a single buffer scheme, which would contain unnecessary objects and decrease memory utilization.

However, the dual buffer approach makes the same object appear in different formats in different buffers at the same time, so we have to maintain internal consistency between two objects denoting the same entity. Currently, we first write back updated or newly created instances from AOT to page buffers in query evaluation. Then we evaluate a query against page buffers. Alternatively, we would have to devise a different search mechanism for different buffers and evaluate the same query against different buffers and integrate the results, which would make the code size of the system rather large.

We describe query evaluation schemes using object buffers and page buffers. Basically, there are two methods for query evaluation, as follows.

Single-buffer evaluation method
(1) The instances newly created or updated associated with the classes specified by the query are searched in the object buffers.
(2) They are flushed from the object buffers to the page buffers.
(3) The query is evaluated against the page buffers.

Dual-buffer evaluation method

(1) The query is evaluated against the object buffers.

(2) The same query is evaluated against the page buffers.

(3) The two results are merged into one.

Jasmine adopts the single-buffer evaluation method. Other systems such as ORION adopt a more sophisticated version of the dual-buffer evaluation method. The single-buffer evaluation method needs to transfer objects from the object buffers to the page buffers. However, the single-buffer evaluation method eliminates the need for dual evaluation programs and makes the system small and processing simple in contrast to the dual-buffer evaluation method. In any case, the combinational use of object buffers and page buffers can support the integration of programming and query facilities at an architecture level.

4.3.4   Support for miscellaneous operations

(1) Class operations are supported. Set-oriented access of classes is translated into a query against the class relation. When the result is scanned, AOT is first searched.

Instantiation is done by invoking the class procedural attribute of REFERENCE which creates instance structures and adds them to AOT with the update flag on. At transaction end, the instances are stored into secondary memory. Classes are similarly created by the instantiate attribute of CLASS which creates a class structure and adds it to AOT.

(2) Database operations, such as session management, database management, and transaction management, are directly implemented by session, database, and transaction operations of the data management subsystem.

(3) Multimedia operations are also supported. Images have pixel data and frame data. Only frame data is stored in secondary memory. At the first display, pixel data is generated from frame data by the if-needed demon. The pixel data is referenced later. Frame data are divided into a subframe of fixed-size pages whose size is maximum. As for graphics, relative address-based data is translated into absolute address-based data by the if-needed demon at first display. Translation from text string data to graphics text data for display is also done by the if-needed demon. Media polymorphism is treated like usual polymorphism. The object expression m.move() is translated into a switch statement whose cases correspond to IMAGE, GRAPHICS, and TEXTS specific move functions.

Direct manipulation of objects is made easier by FIGURE and ARRANGEMENT objects. The procedural attribute of FIGURE searches in ARRANGEMENT objects for an OID of the object whose display area contains the point clicked on by the user. Then the object with the OID is ready for receiving a message. The user can directly manipulate an object by invoking the procedural attribute corresponding to the message. Thus, images, graphics, and texts can be directly manipulated.

Multimedia classes are implemented by bootstrapping the system. They are programmed in Jasmine/C and stored in a separate database from the other kernel classes. This is because multimedia classes can be subject to extension and multimedia data can become voluminous.

(4) Temporary objects have the same internal structures as persistent objects. Although only singleton access is currently permitted to temporary objects from the implementation limitation, no AOT-based search is done with temporary objects, so the application programs can run faster.

4.3.5 Interpreter

The system provides the compiler to improve the efficiency of application execution and provides the interpreter for ease of application development and process of ad hoc queries. The compiler translates the query into extended relational operators as described previously. The interpreter translates the query into extended relational operators and executes them. The interpreter can execute only set-oriented access from the practical point of view. The result of the query is set to a set variable which is referenced by the compiled programs. The user can use the interpreter and the compiled programs in an integrated environment. In particular, since programs are stored as instances, they can be interactively accessed in a set-oriented query. The programs can be invoked interactively after dynamic compilation. The compiler and the interpreter share codes. The interpreter analyzes the input query by using a part of the parser of the compiler. The intermediate codes generated by the interpreter use the functions supplied by the run-time support.

4.3.6 Extensibility

We will summarize the extensibility of Jasmine. The user can flexibly define new data types and associated operations by defining a new class with enumerated and procedural attributes as a subclass of existent system-defined and user-defined classes. The user can extend the object manipulation language just by programming the user-defined function in the language itself without changing the language processor. New access methods for totally-ordered data can be assimilated by supplying the dedicated comparison and range functions of B-tree relations. Other access methods can be incorporated just by programming the tuple layer with almost no modification to the relational layer.

Chapter 5
ARTIFICIAL
INTELLIGENCE
APPLICATIONS

This chapter describes an object-oriented approach to artificial intelligence applications. The content of this section is based on the work [ISHI86] [ISHI87] which was done before an object-oriented database system Jasmine was developed. However, the work has convinced us of the validity of an object-oriented approach to artificial intelligence applications and has led us to the development of Jasmine.

5.1   Introduction

A number of natural language interfaces (NLIs) to database (DB) systems have been developed in an attempt to make DB systems more user-friendly (e.g., [HEND78], [WALT78]). To free the user from the need to know about query languages and DBs, and to allow the user to access DBs in natural language, NLI systems must incorporate a knowledge base that contains knowledge about a domain of discourse, DBs, a query language, and natural language. Moreover, applying NLI systems to new domains requires construction of new knowledge bases for the domains. Recent work has focused on portable NLI systems (e.g., [KAPL84], [MART83]). However, no work has focused on the issues involved in users designing knowledge bases by themselves to transport NLI systems to new domains (One exception, [HEND81], discusses some of them).

Communication between the NLI system and the user requires a model for mutual comprehension, just as dialogues between the human beings do. In order to effectively mediate between the user and the system, a domain model must be represented in terms natural to the concepts the user would employ when thinking about a domain of discourse, instead of semantically poor DB schemata. The user can more easily formulate queries for a conceptually natural domain model than for a DB, and a domain model captures more of the semantics of the domain than a DB. In this respect such models have common goals with semantic data models, e.g., [HAMM81], [MYLO80].

The modeling system for the NLI system must provide the user with mechanisms for abstracting the domain concepts, such as *classification, aggregation, generalization* [SCHR84], and *derivation* [HAMM81] [SHIP81]. This will enable the user to easily build a domain model, make queries based on it, and clearly tell what queries are acceptable, i.e., the *conceptual coverage* [HEND81] of the NLI system.

To guarantee the conceptual naturalness of the domain model, it must be independent of the DB. DB schemata are subject to change for reasons unrelated to the semantics of the domain model, such as space performance issues. To isolate such changes from the domain model, the system must provide the user with a framework for describing a correspondence between the domain model and the underlying DBs. The correspondence, referred to as a *DB mapping*, must be understandable to the user, and flexible enough to buffer DB schema changes and accommodate the user's view. Moreover, the DB mapping must be able to express classification, aggregation, and generalization of the domain concepts. As the DB mapping is used as a knowledge base to translate a domain model query into a DB query, the DB mapping must encapsulate as much domain-specific translation knowledge as possible, from the viewpoint of portability.

The user has to build linguistic knowledge besides the domain model and the DB mapping, to customize an NLI system to a new domain. Thus, the system must provide the user with a framework for describing a vocabulary, i.e., linguistic model, in which to express domain model queries. The linguistic model must be natural and transparent to the user, like the domain model. The system uses the linguistic model as a knowledge base to semantically interpret the user's query. Therefore, the linguistic model must be able to encapsulate as much domain-specific knowledge as possible, so that semantic interpretation can be domain-independent. Moreover, domain-specific knowledge is needed to resolve ambiguities the user's query may contain, depending on the domain. Thus, the user must be able to easily define the linguistic model based on the domain model.

Issues arise from the fact that the knowledge base, including the domain model, linguistic model, and DB mapping, is inherently heuristic; we cannot expect the user to construct a complete knowledge base from the start. Rather, a knowledge base is constructed incrementally. The user must be able to verify that the knowledge base he builds is correct. This can only be determined by testing the knowledge base as it is being constructed. In order to debug the domain model and the linguistic model, the user must be able to tell how a change in the models will influence the semantic interpretation of his query, because the parser uses the models. The user must be able to determine how his query is semantically interpreted. The rules of the parser must therefore be general and clear, and the control of the rules must be simple. Similarly, the translation mechanism must be undestandable enough for the user to debug the DB mapping. Only if all these conditions are satisfied can the user tell how the system understands his query according to the given knowledge base, and refine the knowledge base.

Finally, the users who build knowledge bases are usually neither DB experts nor linguistic experts, but end-user experts in specific domains. Therefore the knowledge base must be as easy form these users to write as possible. The knowledge base must be integrated; the user must be able to describe all kinds of interrelated knowledge in one place, so that he can easily check whether they are consistent. In addition, it is important to provide the user with an environment to support easy and flexible construction of the knowledge base.

This chapter's main point is that a knowledge-based approach is extremely effective for constructing a portable NLI system that satisfies the above design criteria. A knowledge-based approach is to make NLI systems domain-independent by confining domain-specific knowledge needed to process the user's query to the knowledge bases. This chapter discusses an NLI system called *KID* (Knowledge-based Interface to Database systems). KID's portability stems from its knowledge base, called the *world model* (WM). The WM integrates the domain model, linguistic model, and DB mapping. The user can transport KID to a new domain simply by writing a new WM. The encapsulation of all the domain-specific knowledge into the WM makes KID general.

The WM is easy for the user to define and understand. KID's processing of the user's query using the WM is transparent enough to the user to enable easy debugging of the WM. This chapter explains the design of the WM, and KID's knowledge-based processing of user queries using the WM. Section 5.2 gives a brief overview of KID. Section 5.3 presents the design of the WM. Section 5.4 details the semantic interpretation of the user's query using the WM. Section 5.5 explains query translation based on the WM. Section 5.6 summarizes this chapter and compares our work with other related work.

5.2. Sytem Overview

As shown in Figure 5.1, processing of a Japanese-language query is divided into four phases. In the first phase, KID parses the query to make an intermediate meaning structure together with the parse tree. In the translation phase, KID modifies the meaning structure into a WM query and outputs a paraphrased version
of the user's query. If the user confirms the paraphrase, KID translates the WM query into a DB query. In the evaluation phase, KID sends the DB query to a relational[DATE90] database management system (DBMS) such as RDB/V1[MAKI83]; the DBMS evaluates the DB query and sends back the tuples satisfying its conditions. In the last phase, KID shows the results to the user. The WM is used in the first two phases.

We provide a flexible facility for defining domain-specific knowledge in the WM. This facility, called WED (World model EDitor), makes it easier for the user to build and understand the WM, using multiple-windows. WED can be invoked at any time. For example, if KID detects an undefined lexicon in the user's query, the user can edit the WM using WED.

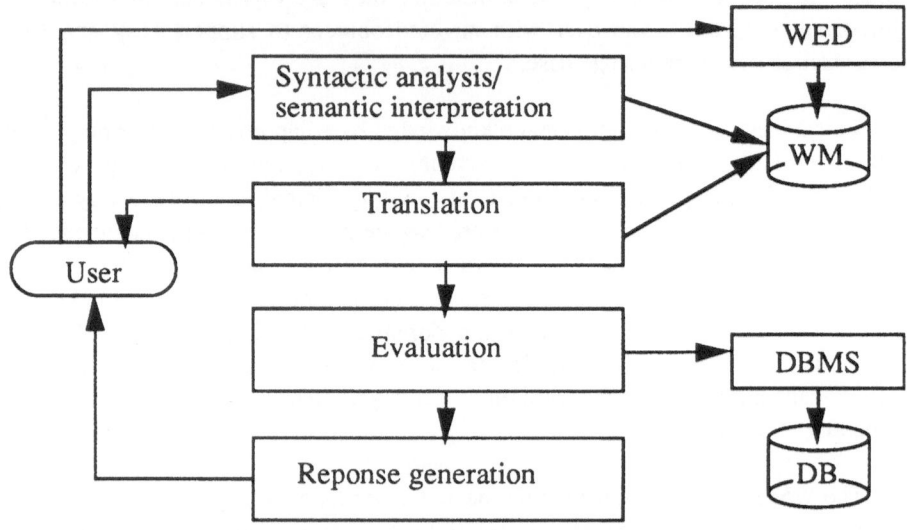

Figure 5.1. An overview of KID.

5.3   World Model Design

To customize KID to a new domain, the user must specify domain-specific knowledge, including the domain model, linguistic model, and DB mapping. The WM provides an integrated framework for describing all of them. The user has only to add new domain-specific knowledge into the WM, to transport KID to a new domain. This section discusses the WM design.

5.3.1 Domain model

5.3.1.1 Classification and aggregation

We now explain how to represent a model of a domain of discourse, called a *domain model*, in the WM. To obtain a conceptually natural domain model, we decided to take an object-oriented approach [BOBR81]. Things and relationships among them in the domain are described in terms of objects and relationships between them. Objects consist of substructures called attributes, which implement properties of and relationships between objects. Moreover, an attribute has several facets, which describe various aspects of that attribute. In particular, the WM objects are called *classes*; they describe properties common to individual objects, called *instances*. Domain concepts are divided into classes. The WM classes as a whole represent a model of a domain of discourse just sufficiently. Hence the user can see the conceptual coverage of KID by browsing in the WM using WED.

Figure 5.2 illustrates parts of class definitions in a merchandising domain. The values of the attribute *Attribute*, as described by the values of its facet *value*, indicate user-defined attributes. For example, the class SALE has Retailer, Commodity, Sales, and Price, as its user-defined attributes. The value of the attribute *Level* distinguishes among instances, classes, and metaclasses (i.e., classes of classes). For example, SALE is on a class-level. The facet *class* of the user-defined attribute indicates the class for the value domain of the attribute. Another example, the domain class of the attribute Retailer of SALE is RETAILER. Attribute names must be unique within a class; different classes may have the same attribute names (see RETAILER and FACTORY). However, attributes are to always be referenced by prefixing class names, so we can avoid introducing extraneous notions such as *internal* and *external function names*[SHIP81], i.e., attribute names.

```
SALE
    Super               value       ENTITY
    Class               value       NONPRIMITIVE
    Level               value       classlevel
    Attribute           value       Retailer Commodity
                                    Sales Price
    Retailer            class       RETAILER
                        storage     SALE_RETAILER_MAPPING
    Commodity           class       COMMODITY
                        storage
                                SALE_COMMODITY_MAPPING
    Sales               class       SALES
                        storage  SALE_SALES_MAPPING
                        multiple    yes
    Price               class       COMMODITY
                        storage
                                SALE_COMMODITY_MAPPING
```

Figure 5.2. Parts of world class model definitions.

RETAILER

Super	value	ENTITY
Class	value	NONPRIMITIVE
Level	value	classlevel
Attribute	value	Code Name Address
Key	value	Code
Return	value	Code Name
Code	class	RETAILER_CODE
	storage	RETAILER_CODE_MAPPING
	mandatory	yes
Name	class	RETAILER_NAME
	storage	RETAILER_NAME_MAPPING
Address	class	RETAILER_ADDRESS
	storage	
		RETAILER_ADDRESS_MAPPING

FACTORY

Super	value	ENTITY
Class	value	NONPRIMITIVE
Level	value	classlevel
Attribute	value	Code Name Address
Key	value	Code
Return	value	Code Name
Code	class	FACTORY_CODE
	storage	FACTORY_CODE_MAPPING
	mandatory	yes
Name	class	FACTORY_NAME
	storage	FACTORY_NAME_MAPPING
Address	class	FACTORY_ADDRESS
	storage	
		FACTORY_ADDRESS_MAPPING

Figure 5.2. Parts of world class model definitions(continued).

RETAILER_CODE

Super	value	CODE
	storage	RETAILER_CODE_MAPPING
Class	value	PRIMITIVE
Level	value	classlevel
Inverse	value	RETAILER
GET_VALUE	method	retailer_code_get_value
NORMALIZE_VALUE	method	retailer_code_normalize

RETAILER_NAME

Super	value	NAME
	storage	RETAILER_NAME_MAPPING
Class	value	PRIMITIVE
Level	value	classlevel
Inverse	value	RETAILER
GET_VALUE	method	retailer_name_get_value
NORMALIZE_VALUE	method	retailer_name_normalize

COMMODITY

Super	value	ENTITY
Class	value	NONPRIMITIVE
Level	value	classlevel
Attribute	value	Code Name
Key	value	Code
Code	class	COMMODITY_CODE
	storage	COMMODITY_CODE_MAPPING
	mandatory	yes
Name	class	COMMODITY_NAME
	storage	COMMODITY_NAME_MAPPING

BEER

Super	value	COMMODITY
	derivation	BEER_DERIVATION
Class	value	NONPRIMITIVE
Level	value	classlevel
Attribute	value	Code Name
Key	value	Code

Figure 5.2. Parts of world class model definitions (continued).

System-defined attributes also describe several characteristics of a class. First, key attributes can be specified by the attribute *Key*, such as Code of RETAILER. The value of the key attribute identifies the instances of the class uniquely. Moreover, the user can control the display of the attribute value; the attribute *Return* indicates which attributes to return when referenced (see RETAILER). Furthermore, the inverse of the attribute can be defined (see RETAILER_NAME). The attribute *Inverse* is used to make inferences in semantic interpretation of the user's query.

In addition to *value* and *class*, facets provide an attribute with various aspects. The facet *multiple* distinguishes between single-valued and multiple-valued attributes. For example, Sales of SALE is multiple-valued. The facet *mandatory* specifies a non-null attribute. Key attributes must be non-null. Knowledge specified by system-defined facets (e.g., multiple) and attributes (e.g., Key, Return) is used in query translation.

Figure 5.3 represents a part of the merchandising domain model graphically. Ovals denote classes, and arrows the relationships between them. Solid arrows depict attribute relationships, and broken arrows super-sub relationships. Leaf nodes and internal nodes of a graphical representation of the WM are called *primitive* and *nonprimitive* classes, respectively. They are distinguished by their metaclasses, i.e., by the attribute Class. For example, SALE, RETAILER, and COMMODITY are nonprimitive; ADDRESS, NAME, and RETAILER_NAME are primitive. The WM classes include *complex objects* [HASK82], such as SALE; the WM classes allow arbitrarily nested aggregation.

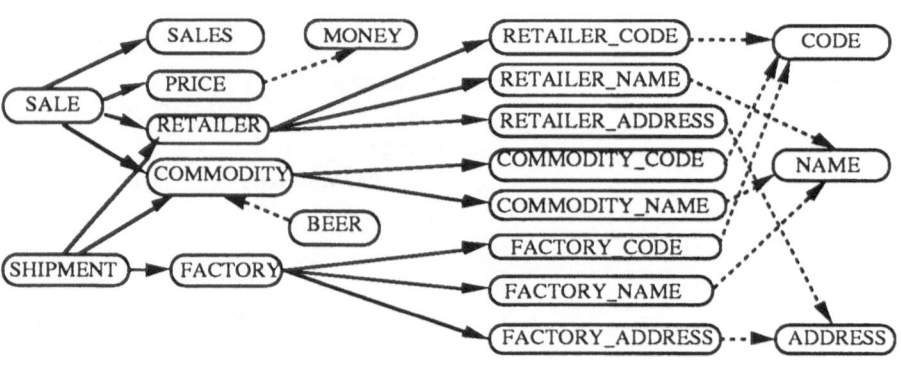

Figure 5.3. A graphical representation of the domain model.

5.3.1.2 Generalization

To enhance the naturalness of the domain model, we introduce *generalization*, which enables the user to easily define classes similar to existing ones with a few incremental changes. The newly-defined classes are called *subclasses*, and the old ones are called *superclasses*. The relationship is called a *super-sub relationship*. A superclass is denoted by the attribute *Super*, by which the subclass inherits all the attributes of that superclass. For example, BEER inherits Code and Name from COMMODITY (see Figure 5.2). The attribute Super introduces generalization hierarchies in the WM.

The need for generalization emerges naturally during model design. We adopt the heuristic method of model design, which cannot be detailed here due to space limitations. By this method, classes and their relationships are identified, paying close attention to nouns and verbs in fragments of the user's natural language queries collected before knowledge base design. For example, sentence fragments "the name of the retailer" and "the name of the factory" make RETAILER-->RETAILER_NAME and FACTORY-->FACTORY_NAME parts of the WM. NAME is constructed as a common superclass of RETAILER_NAME and FACTORY_NAME (see Figure 5.3). Furthermore, NAME is a subclass of the system-defined class JSTRING, a string of Japanese-language characters. FACTORY and RETAILER are subclasses of the system-defined class ENTITY, the superclass of all the WM classes (see Figure 5.2).

5.3.1.3 Derivation

We provide the WM with a derivation mechanism to extend the naturalness of the WM. Derivation enables the user to see the same information in several ways, which helps the user to define new views of the domain model. In KID, derivation enables the user to define new attributes or classes by restricting or combining existing attributes or classes. The derivation is specified by the WM query language, as explained in Section 5.5. The derived classes or attributes can be accessed by the same interface as the basic classes, i.e., classes which have any DB mapping. The user specifies any derivation as a kind of class in the facet *derivation* (see Super of BEER in Figure 5. 2). Classes or attributes can be derived not only from the basic classes or attributes, but also from other derived classes or attributes.

An example is when we model a sentence fragment "sell in some place" in the merchandising domain. Suppose that the WM has no direct relationships between SALE and ADDRESS. The user can adapt his linguistic view to the WM by deriving the attribute Location for SALE, specifying Address of Retailer of SALE (see SALE_LOCATION_DERIVATION in Figure 5.4). BEER_DERIVATION shows that BEER can be derived as a subclass of COMMODITY by restricting its Code value.

SALE_LOCATION_DERIVATION

Super	value	DERIVATION
Class	value	METACLASS
Level	value	classlevel
Get	value	display SALE:Retailer:Address

BEER_DERIVATION

Super	value	DERIVATION
Class	value	METACLASS
Level	value	classlevel
Get	value	display COMMODITY where COMMODITY:Code<= 103

Figure 5.4. Derivation description classes.

5.3.1.4 Integration

The WM classes can do more than model a domain of discourse. The user can also describe the DB mapping and linguistic correspondence in the WM classes. The integration of all the relevant knowledge into one place, i.e., class, enables the user to easily write it and check its consistency. The DB mapping can be statically described in the facet *storage* of the attribute of the WM class (see Retailer of SALE in Figure 5.2). For the linguistic knowledge, the user can define the vocabulary based on the domain model, i.e., classes, and see what lexicons are allocated to the classes, by using WED. Dynamic properties, such as a procedure to get a required value out of input text, can also be described as methods [BOBR81] in the WM classes. For example, the parser can put the values into the instances by sending them a message "GET_VALUE" (see RETAILER_NAME in Figure 5.2). The WM differs significantly from *semantic data models* (e.g.,[HAMM81]) in that they describe only static properties of objects.

5.3.2 Linguistic model

To apply KID to a new domain, the user must define knowledge about natural language. The knowledge, called the Linguistic Model (LM), is used when the parser semantically interprets the user's query. The user expresses his query with the LM. The LM consists of definitions of lexicons and relationships between them. Lexicons can be defined by associating them with the WM classes. The relationships between the lexicons can be viewed as identical to those between the associated classes. A *case frame* [BARR81] of a verb is denoted by a set of all attributes of the associated class. For example, the noun "retailer" and the verb "sell" refer to the classes RETAILER and SALE, respectively. The case frame of the verb "sell" is a set (Retailer Commodity Sales Price). The user can tell how to express his query by looking up the lexicons allocated to the classes, using WED.

Our approach of defining the LM based on the WM classes makes the LM more natural in several ways. First, the LM, or case frames, can be represented succinctly by use of generalization of the classes. For example, when we model two sentences "sell beer" and "sell wine," usually we must define a separate case frame for each of them, such as (... Beer ...) and (... Wine ...). However, if BEER and WINE are to be defined as subclasses of COMMODITY, then the case frame alone, including the Commodity case, can represent the same knowledge as represented by the two separate case frames. The LM also supports user linguistic views different from the given WM classes, by derivation.

Further, the LM allows some ambiguity in the user's natural language queries. Ambiguities arise from the need for the naturalness of the LM. It is a natural language phenomenon that generic nouns are specialized by modifications, such as noun phrases and clauses; the nouns themselves should be defined to correspond to classes which are as general as possible. For example, it is natural to associate the proper noun "Tokyo" with ADDRESS, but not with RETAILER_ADDRESS or FACTORY_ADDRESS. However, if the noun "Tokyo" is referred to in the user's query, the class for the noun must be specialized to either RETAILER_ADDRESS or FACTORY_ADDRESS according to the context, to unambiguously answer the query. These ambiguities can be resolved by semantic interpretation using the LM, as discussed in Section 5.4.

5.3.3 Mapping

In KID, the user defines the (DB) mapping by associating the WM classes with the relations [DATE90] in the DB. The user can make the domain model and linguistic model in the WM independent of the DB by encapsulating most of the domain-specific translation knowledge into the mapping. Thus, the mapping prevents DB schema changes irrelevant to the semantics of the WM from affecting the naturalness of the WM. Moreover, the mapping enables the user to flexibly express classification, aggregation, and generalization of classes.

We choose to make the mapping description formalism close to the relational query language, rather than devise a new language specifically for the mapping, because the user can easily specify which relations to retrieve with a nonprocedural query language. This makes the mapping understandable and flexible. In addition to a one-to-one mapping between the WM classes and the DB relations, the user can specify nontrivial mappings, including multiple target fields and joins[DATE90]. The user specifies the mapping as a kind of class in the facet storage of the attribute. For example,

SALE_RETAILER_MAPPING in Figure 5.5 shows the mapping description class for Retailer of SALE. Here, suffixes _TBL and _FLD denote table (relation) and field (column) respectively. The mapping as the value of the attribute *Get* of the class specifies that when Retailer of SALE is referenced, RETAILER_CODE_FLD and RETAILER_NAME_FLD of RETAILER_TBL are returned by joining RETAILER_TBL and SALE_TBL.

SALE_RETAILER_MAPPING

Super	value	MAPPING
Class	value	METACLASS
Level	value	classlevel
Get	value	get
		RETAILER_TBL:RETAILER_CODE_FLD
		RETAILER_TBL:RETAILER_NAME_FLD
		where
		RETAILER_TBL:RETAILER_CODE_FLD =
		SALE_TBL:SALE_RETAILER_FLD

RETAILER_NAME_MAPPING

Super	value	MAPPING
Class	value	METACLASS
Level	value	classlevel
Get	value	get
		RETAILER_TBL:RETAILER_NAME_FLD

Figure 5.5.   Mapping description classes.

Although the user can choose his own mapping approach, we advocate the following top-down approach, in which the DB schemata are defined based on the given WM classes. First, consider classification and aggregation. The user should simply allocate one relation to one class. Suppose that we give a relation R1 to a class C1. If the domain class for an attribute A1 of C1 is primitive, then the mapping for A1 is to be a field F1 of R1. Otherwise, another relation R2 is to be given to the nonprimitive domain class C2 for A1 of C1. Moreover, a field F2 of R1 is to be defined as a *foreign key* [DATE90] for R2. The mapping for A1 is to return fields of R2 by joining R1 and R2 by F2 of R1 and the key field of R2. For example, we define a relation SALE_TBL with a foreign key SALE_RETAILER_FLD for SALE, and a relation RETAILER_TBL with a key RETAILER_CODE_FLD for RETAILER. Moreover, we write RETAILER_NAME_MAPPING for Name of RETAILER, and SALE_RETAILER_MAPPING for Retailer of SALE (see Figure 5.5).

For generalization, we recommend that the user write in the attribute Super of the class either of two mappings: (1) a mapping restricting some fields of the relation for the superclass, (2) a mapping joining the relation for the superclass and another relation for the subclass including the fields for subclass-specific attributes and the common key fields with the relation for the superclass. For example, one way to define the mapping for BEER specifies the relation for COMMODITY (i.e., COMMODITY_TBL) by restricting its key field (i.e., COMMODITY_CODE_FLD). Another way is to join COMMODITY_TBL and the separate relation for BEER ("BEER_TBL," including a field "BEER_CAN_SIZE_FLD" and the key field "BEER_CODE_FLD") by COMMODITY_CODE_FLD and BEER_CODE_FLD.

5.4 Semantic Interpretation

5.4.1 Issues in parsing

The parser analyzes the user's Japanese-language request to extract its meaning. Analysis is based on the modification relationships between phrases such as noun phrases or verb phrases. In general, analyzing a sentence grammatically is called *syntactic analysis*; analysis using the meanings of lexicons is called *semantic analysis* [BARR81].

The user's request often has both *syntactic* and *semantic ambiguities*[KAPL84]. Syntactic ambiguities occur when there is more than one possible modification relationship between the phrases. For example, in the request "Tokyo no biiru wo uru mise no namae wa ?" ("What is the name of the retailer which sells beer in Tokyo ?"), the noun phrase "Tokyo no" (in Tokyo) may modify either a noun phrase "biiru wo" (beer), a noun phrase "mise no" (of the retailer) or a verb phrase "uru" (sells) syntactically. Semantic ambiguities may also arise when phrases have multiple meanings. For example, the noun phrase "Tokyo no" (in Tokyo) corresponds to a particular address, but its meaning should be either a "factory-address" or a "retailer-address" depending on the context in the merchandising domain. To resolve these ambiguities, we need semantic knowledge about the domain.

There are two extremes when using semantics in parsing. One extreme is to divide the syntactic and semantic analysis into two completely separate steps, e.g., [MART83]. This can lead to a combinatorial explosion in the number of possible parses. The opposite extreme is *semantic grammar* [BARR81], where the semantic information is embedded in the grammatical categories. This makes no distinction between domain-specific knowledge and general knowledge, so the semantic grammar-based parser (e.g., [HEND78]) is less transportable. Thus, we took the middle approach.

5.4.2 Our approach

Our goal is to semantically interpret the user's query, keeping the parser domain-independent, and at the same time preventing a combinatorial explosion in the number of possible parses. Syntactic and semantic analysis proceeds incrementally. A rule in the KID parser consists of both syntactic and semantic parts, including checks and actions. The possible modification relationships between the phrases must pass the syntactic and semantic checks. If both of the checks are successful, then the syntactic and semantic actions deterministically produce the partial parse tree and meaning for the modification, respectively. This reduces the number of possible intermediate parses drastically, which prevents a combinatorial explosion.

We can make the parser domain-independent by encapsulating into the WM the domain-specific knowledge used by semantic checks and actions, and by restricting the parser's knowledge source to the WM. That is, the semantic checks on the modification relationships between the phrases are based only on the relationships between the classes for the nouns or verbs in the phrases given by the LM. If the classes are connected by an attribute or super-sub relationship, then the phrases are unified into one phrase, called a *unified phrase*, with the meaning made by consulting the WM only. This makes the parsing rules clear and general.

5.4.2.1 Meaning representation

We use the WM not only as a knowledge base for semantic interpretation, but also as a meaning representation for the user's query. Semantic interpretation identifies the WM classes in the user's query, instantiates them, and makes a network of the instances isomorphic to the WM classes as a meaning structure of the input. This isomorphic structure enables the user to clearly verify the results of semantic interpretation. During processing, the parser gets the values required for later processing (e.g., making the qualification in the WM query) from the input text, and puts them into the instances. The surface structures of the phrases vary from one class to another, so the user has to specify individual procedures for each class. However, if the user writes class-specific methods under the same name "GET_ VALUE" in the WM classes (see RETAILER_NAME in Figure 5.2), then the parser can do these individual tasks "uniformly" by sending all the instances the message "GET_VALUE"; this object-oriented feature of the WM keeps the parser domain-independent.

The central class in the meaning, corresponding to the root in the network, is called the *conceptual class*. The class which the phrase denotes literally is called the *syntactic class*. The parser integrates subtrees into a larger tree. The meaning, syntactic class, and conceptual class are attached to the integrated tree by combining the counterparts of the subtrees (see Figure 5.6).

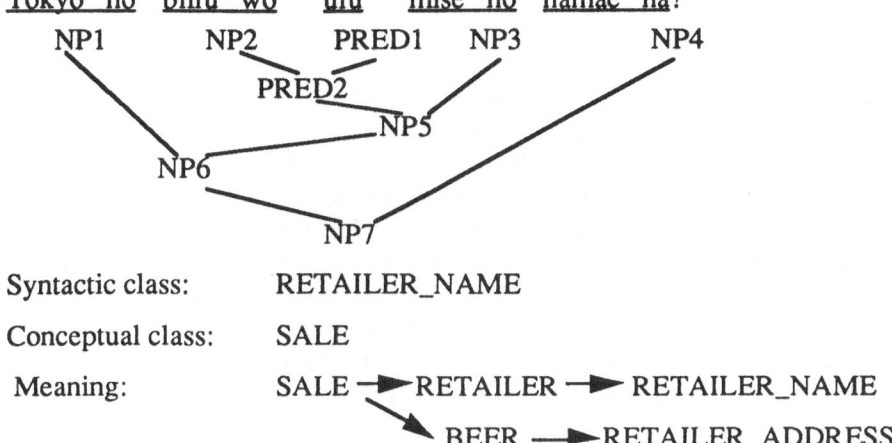

Figure 5.6. An example of parsing.

5.4.2.2 Principles for using the WM

We present two general principles the parser uses when it consults the WM. They help to resolve ambiguities in the user's query naturally and efficiently.

(1) Specialization principle

If two classes in a generalization hierarchy are given, the rule prefers the subclass to the superclass (e.g., RETAILER_NAME in a NAME/RETAILER_NAME hierarchy). This principle can resolve the semantic ambiguities of the phrases naturally. This principle is based by the general language phenomenon that a concept is specialized by modifications.

(2) Centralization principle

If two classes connected by an attribute relationship are given, the rule prefers the "whole" class to the "part" class (e.g., SALE in SALE/RETAILER attribute relationship). This helps to efficiently resolve syntactic ambiguities by determining the conceptual focus, i.e., the conceptual class. From the viewpoint of efficiency, semantic checks are done by using the syntactic or conceptual classes which index the meaning structure, rather than by exhaustive search of the meaning.

5.4.2.3   Rules

The rules are classified into two groups according to the types of relationships between the WM classes which they handle: identification rules for super-sub relationships and connection rules for user-defined attribute relationships. The rules are further specialized according to the syntactic patterns to which they apply. Like the identification rules, the connection rules are general and domain-independent in that they treat all user-defined attributes in the same manner. The rules identify the modification relationships among the phrases with the relationships among the This enables the user to intuitively and clearly grasp the process of semantic interpretation. Given the WM, the user can predict the results of semantic interpretation of his query, by knowing these rules plus the above two principles. A few typical rules follow:

(1) NP-NP identification rule

This rule applies to syntactic patterns such as a noun phrase (NP) with the postposition (PP) "ga" (indicating a subject or an object of a sentence, depending on the context) followed by an NP with the PP "no" (ownership or a sentence subject). If two classes for the two NPs are in a hierarchy, the two NPs are unified into one NP. The classes of the unified NP (meaning, syntactic, and conceptual classes) are the subclass, by the Specialization principle. For example, consider the following:

> "...kakaku ga 300 en no..."
>   (price)   (300)(yen)
> ("...price is 300 yen...")

Here the NP "kakaku ga" (price) and the NP "300 yen no" (yen is the Japanese currency) refer to the classes PRICE and MONEY, respectively. They are in a super-sub relationship, so the NPs are unified. The classes are all specialized to PRICE.

(2) NP-NP connection rule

This rule applies to syntactic patterns such as an NP with the PP "no" followed by an NP with a PP of any kind, such as "ga", "wa" (a subject or an object of a sentence), or "wo" (a sentence object). If the associated classes are directly connected by an attribute relationship, such as SALE and RETAILER, or indirectly via super-sub relationships, such as RETAILER and ADDRESS, then the two NPs are unified into one NP. The syntactic class of the unified NP is that of the second NP, because the latter phrase is syntactically dominant in a Japanese-language sentence. The conceptual class is determined by the Centralization principle. The meaning is made by merging the meanings of the two NPs. All these classes are specialized by the Specialization principle as required. For example, consider the following:

> "...mise   no namae wa..."
> (retailer)(of)(name)
> ("...the name of the retailer is...")

Here the NP "mise no" (of the retailer) and the NP "namae wa" (the name) correspond to RETAILER and NAME, respectively. Because RETAILER has NAME as its attribute, the two NPs are unified into one NP. The syntactic class of the unified NP is specialized to RETAILER_NAME. The conceptual class is set to RETAILER and the merged meaning becomes RETAILER-->RETAILER_NAME.

(3) PREDP connection rule

This rule applies to syntactic patterns such as a series of NPs followed by a predicate phrase (PREDP). If the class for the PREDP has each class for the NPs as
its attribute, then all the phrases are unified into one PREDP. Moreover, if the PREDP is followed by an NP and if their classes are connected by an attribute relationship, then the two phrases are unified into one NP. The classes of the unified phrase are determined, as in (2). For example, consider the following:

> "...Fujitsuya ga biiru wo uru..."
> (retailer name) (beer) (sells)
> ("...Fujitsuya sells beer...")

Here the NP "Fujitsuya ga" (a particular retailer name), the NP "biiru wo" (beer), and the PREDP "uru" (sells) refer to RETAILER_NAME, BEER, and SALE, respectively. The modification relationship between the NP "biiru wo" and the PREDP holds, because SALE has BEER as its attribute. The relationship between the NP "Fujitsuya ga" and the PREDP does not hold, because SALE does not have RETAILER_NAME as its attribute. However, here the parser uses a heuristic; the system infers that when the user mentions the retailer's name, the user associates it with the retailer itself. The system can make this inference by knowing that the inverse class of RETAILER_NAME is RETAILER. The system takes RETAILER as the conceptual class of the NP "Fujitsuya ga." Further, SALE has RETAILER as its attribute, so the modification relationship between the NP and PREDP holds. Thus, the three phrases are unified into one PREDP; the syntactic and conceptual classes are both set to SALE and the meaning becomes:

        SALE-->RETAILER-->RETAILER_NAME.
          \\-->BEER

5.4.2.4 Control of rules

To make it easier to debug the WM, we keep control of the rules as simple as possible, by taking a *priority-based approach*[BARR81]. Each rule is given a priority according to the strength of relationships between the classes for phrases handled by that rule. In general, identification rules are given higher priority than connection rules, because the super-sub relationship is stronger than the attribute relationship from the viewpoint of similarity. The parser applies the rules with the highest priority to the user's utterance, from left to right. If the conditions of a rule are satisfied, then the actions are performed; otherwise the rules with the next highest priority are tried. This continues until the parser finds a rule whose condition is satisfied. After an action is performed by a rule, the parser applies the highest priority rule from the beginning of the input again. The parser continues this process until there are no rules that apply. If the parser has a unified tree at that time, the parsing succeeds, otherwise it fails. This priority-based control results in a unique parse tree and meaning, if parsing is successful.

Simple control of the rules makes the parser robust, so it can accept even ungrammatical queries. The user cannot always be expected to make a complete and correct query. Robustness is vital, to make the system user-friendly. Thus, we write rules that can handle patterns the standard rules cannot, and then give them lower priority than the standard rules.

5.4.2.5 How the rules work

To illustrate how the rules work, consider the following query:

        "Tokyo   no biiru wo uru   mise   no namae wa ?"
        (address)(of)(beer) (sells)(retailer)(of)(name)
        ("What is the name of the retailer which sells beer in Tokyo?")

This query has some syntactic ambiguities. The NP "Tokyo no" (in Tokyo, a particular address denoting the class ADDRESS) has three possible NPs that it could modify: "biiru wo" (beer, BEER), "mise no" (of the retailer, RETAILER) or "namae wa" (the name, NAME). The PREDP "uru" (sells, SALE) has two possible NPs to modify:

"mise no" (of the retailer) and "namae wa" (the name). The query also has two semantic ambiguities; "Tokyo no" (ADDRESS) and "namae wa" (NAME) could be specialized. The rules resolve all these ambiguities as explained below.

First, the PREDP connection rule unifies PREDP1 "uru" (sells) and NP2 "biiru wo" (beer) into PREDP2 (see Figure 5.6), because SALE has BEER as its attribute. Then, the PREDP connection rule unifies PREDP2 and NP3 "mise no" (of the retailer) into NP5, because SALE, the syntactic class of PREDP2, has RETAILER as its attribute. This also resolves the syntactic ambiguity of PREDP1 "uru" (sells); PREDP1 modifies NP3 "mise no" (of the retailer). Next, the NP-NP connection rule unifies NP1 "Tokyo no" (in Tokyo) and NP5 into NP6, because RETAILER, the syntactic class of NP5, has ADDRESS as its attribute. This resolves both the syntactic and semantic ambiguities of NP1 "Tokyo no" (in Tokyo). NP1 modifies NP3 "mise no" (of the retailer), and ADDRESS, the class of NP1, is specialized to RETAILER_ADDRESS. Finally, the NP-NP connection rule unifies NP6 and NP4 "namae wa" (the name) into one complete sentence because RETAILER, the syntactic class of NP6, has NAME as its attribute. This resolves the semantic ambiguity of NP4 "namae wa" (the name); NAME is specialized to RETAILER_NAME. Figure 5.6 illustrates the parse tree together with the classes.

5.5 Query Translation

The meaning structure produced by semantic interpretation of the user's query is translated into a WM query, then the WM query is translated into a DB query. In this section, we discuss the WM query language, and our approach to translation.

5.5.1 WM query language

The WM query language basically consists of the target list, which specifies what data to return, and the qualification list, which specifies the conditions the data must satisfy. For example, "What is the name of the retailer which sells beer in Tokyo ?" is translated into the following WM query:

> display SALE:Retailer:Name SALE:Beer
> where SALE:Retailer:Address="TOKYO"

The keyword *display* is followed by the target list, and the keyword *where* by the qualification list. The expression basically consists of a class name, followed by arbitrary number of attribute names with ":" between them. The ":" notation corresponds to the "." notation, i.e., *functional join* [TSUR84] or a *functional composition*

[SHIP81]. The ":" operator can specify complex objects, i.e., aggregation, to any desired detail. It can also accommodate property inheritance, i.e., generalization, such as BEER:Name.

Further, the user can express WM queries including joins, i.e., entity-joins[TSUR84], nested queries, and aggregate functions with "group by" and "having" clauses[DATE90]. For example, the user's query "Which retailer sells the most ?" is translated into the following WM query:

> display SALE:Retailer
> groupby SALE:Retailer:Code
> having SUM(SALE:Sales)
>   = MAX(SUM(SALE:Sales)
>   groupby SALE:Retailer:Code)

Here the knowledge that the key attribute of RETAILER is Code makes the expression in the *groupby* clause. Moreover, the knowledge that Sales of SALE is multiple-valued puts the aggregate function *SUM* before SALE:Sales in the *having* clause. In this way, the knowledge described in the WM classes is used to process the user query.

5.5.2 Our approach to translation

Several issues arise in translating a WM query. The translation must be done correctly according to the domain-specific knowledge. Besides basic mapping, the WM query expressions may involve any level of nested derivation, generalization, and functional joins in any combination(e.g., SALE:Beer:Name). There is a large gap between the WM query including such complex expressions and the query against the "flat" relations; the gap must be bridged to correctly translate the query.

Therefore, we adopt as the translation mechanism a *rule-based*[BARR81] scheme whose advantages are modularity, uniformity, and naturalness. We can divide the translation task into primitive subtasks, each performing only one function, such as generalization, derivation, or functional join, and allocate one subtask to one rule.

A second issue arises from the fact that the user defines mappings by himself. The translation mechanism must be undestandable enough for the user to easily verify the correctness of a mapping that he builds heuristically. The rule-based mechanism also solves this problem, because it is appropriate for explicit description of behavioral knowledge. That it is modular and uniform helps the user to understand the translation process. To help the user debug the mapping, we provide trace/break functions as basic features of the rule-based mechanism. They can be invoked at any time. The user can use this facility to see the translation process step by step. It is also effective for rule debugging.

We want the WM to be independent of the DBMS in addition to the DB, so that we can extend KID to different DBMSs. We make a clear separation between the rules, i.e., knowledge about a particular query language, and their control, i.e., the interpreter. This way the user can control the rule contents. The user has only to modify or replace the rules themselves to apply KID to a new DBMS.

In addition to the mapping and the derivation, the translation must be done based on the domain-specific knowledge. The representation of a value in the expression of the WM query does not necessarily agree with its counterpart of the DB query. For example, while the value of RETAILER_CODE is represented as an integer in the WM, the corresponding value is a string in the DB. The translation must take such class-specific kinds of knowledge into account. On the other hand, we must provide a general framework for describing such knowledge, to maintain portability. This can be done by integrating object-oriented features with the rule-oriented scheme[BOBR81]. The user can give a common name to class-specific methods for value conversion. Then, the system can activate domain-specific translation "uniformly" by sending a message using the common name.

5.5.3 Translation rules

Query translation is done cooperatively by several "rulesets," which are collections of rules that perform coherent tasks. Rulesets are organized for key clauses of the WM query language. Target-, groupby-, having-, and qualification rulesets process display-, groupby-, having-, and where clauses, respectively. Each ruleset shares two workspaces, one for WM query input and one for DB query output. The rulesets look in the WM query workspace for expressions to which they apply. If any expressions are found, the rulesets translate them to modify the workspaces. Each rule basically transforms the ":" notation in the WM query, using the relevant knowledge in the WM class, such as a mapping or derivation. A mapping modifies the DB query workspace, a derivation the WM query workspace. Each rule is applied repeatedly until the WM query workspace is empty, at which point the translation process terminates. We describe the principal functions of each ruleset below.

5.5.3.1 Target ruleset

This ruleset processes the target list in the WM query. The rules include:

(1) mapping

If the ":" notation includes any mapping, the contents are added to the DB query workspace. The target and qualification parts of the mapping are merged into the corresponding parts of the DB query workspace. For example,

    (WM query workspace)   (DB query workspace)
      RETAILER:Name --> RETAILER_TBL:RETAILER_NAME_FLD

(2) derivation

If the ":" notation includes any derivation, i.e., derived class or attribute, then the contents are merged into the WM query workspace. For example,

    (WM query workspace)
        BEER:Code
  -->   COMMODITY:Code where COMMODITY:Code<=103

(3) complex object

If a complex object whose attribute Super has neither a mapping nor derivation appears with no attributes specified in the expression, then it is expanded into its component classes to merge into the WM query workspace. However, if the complex object has the attribute Return, expansion is performed according to its value. For example,

    (WM query workspace)
        RETAILER
  -->   RETAILER:Code RETAILER:Name

(4) generalization

If the ":" notation has any property inheritance, then the mapping or derivation specified in the attribute Super of the class, i.e., subclass, is added to the DB or WM query workspace, respectively. The mapping or derivation in the attribute of the superclass is also added. For example, suppose that two separate relations are given for COMMODITY/BEER generalization, and the mapping joining the two relations and the mapping "get COMMODITY_TBL:COMMODITY_NAME_FLD" are specified for Super of BEER and Name of COMMODITY, respectively:

```
(WM query workspace)   (DB query workspace)
BEER:Name     --> COMMODITY-TBL:COMMODITY_NAME_FLD
              where COMMODITY_TBL:COMMODITY_CODE_FLD
                  = BEER_TBL:BEER_CODE_FLD
```

(5) functional join

A long expression including more than one ":" operator, i.e., functional join, is reduced one step at a time. If the ":" notation has any mapping, then it is merged into the DB query workspace. If it has any derivation, it is merged into the WM query workspace. In the former case, the resultant class for the ":" notation, i.e., the domain class for the attribute, is added to the WM query workspace. For example,

```
(WM query workspace)   (DB query workspace)
SALE:Retailer:Name --> where SALE_TBL:SALE_RETAILER_FLD
                            = RETAILER_TBL:RETAILER_CODE_FLD
--> RETAILER:Name
```

(6) aggregate function

If the expression contains an aggregate function (e.g.,SUM, MAX), then the parameter of the function is translated by recursively applying the target ruleset. For example, suppose the mapping "get SALE_TBL:SALE_SALES_FLD" for Sales of SALE:

```
(WM query workspace)   (DB query workspace)
SUM(SALE:Sales)      --> SUM(SALE_TBL:SALE_SALES_FLD)
```

5.5.3.2 Groupby ruleset

This ruleset processes the groupby clause. Making key fields of the DB query out of the key expressions of the WM query is similar to processing the target list. For example, suppose the mapping "get RETAILER_TBL:RETAILER_CODE_FLD" for Code of RETAILER:

```
(WM query workspace)   (DB query workspace)
SALE:Retailer:Code     --> RETAILER_TBL:RETAILER_CODE_FLD
                        where SALE_TBL:SALE_RETAILER_FLD
                            = RETAILER_TBL:RETAILER_CODE_FLD
```

5.5.3.3 Having ruleset

In the having clause, the aggregate function is compared either with a constant or with the result of the nested query. For the nested query, target-, groupby-, having-, and qualification rulesets are invoked recursively. For example,

```
(WM query workspace)              (DB query workspace)
SUM(SALE:Sales)          --> SUM(SALE_TBL:SALE_SALES_FLD)
=MAX( SUM(SALE:Sales)     =   MAX(SUM(SALE_TBL:SALE_SALES_FLD)
  groupby SALE:Retailer:Code)     where SALE_TBL:SALE_RETAILER_FLD
                                      =RETAILER_TBL:RETAILER_CODE_FLD
                                  groupby
                                      RETAILER_TBL:RETAILER_CODE_FLD)
```

5.5.3.4 Qualification ruleset

This ruleset processes the where clause. Most of its functions are in common with the target ruleset, except that it must convert the value, and handle logical- and comparative operators and nested queries. The ruleset always sends the predefined message "NORMALIZE_VALUE" to convert the value. The codes for the message are specified optionally by the user for each class (see RETAILER_CODE in Figure 5.2). This makes the translation domain-independent. For example,

```
(WM query workspace)              (DB query workspace)
RETAILER:Code=100 -->
                          (send RETAILER_CODE  "NORMALIZE VALUE" 100)
                          --> RETAILER_TBL:RETAILER_CODE_FLD="100"
```

5.5.3.5 Translation example

The first WM query example illustrated in Section 5.5.1 is translated by the rulesets explained above into the following DB query:

```
get RETAILER_TBL:RETAILER_CODE_FLD
      RETAILER_TBL:RETAILER_NAME_FLD
      COMMODITY_TBL:COMMODITY_CODE_FLD
      COMMODITY_TBL:COMMODITY_NAME_FLD
 where SALE_TBL:SALE_RETAILER_FLD
        =RETAILER_TBL:RETAILER_CODE_FLD
   and  SALE_TBL:SALE_COMMODITY_FLD
        =COMMODITY_TBL:COMMODITY_CODE_FLD
   and  COMMODITY_TBL:COMMODITY_CODE_FLD<="103"
   and  RETAILER_TBL:RETAILER_ADDRESS_FLD="TOKYO"
```

5. 6 Conclusion

5.6.1 Related work

KID is the result of the integration of work on natural language understanding from the AI field, work on data modeling from the DB field, and work on object notions from the programming language field.

There has been a major attempt to construct portable NLI systems, such as CO-OP[KAPL84], TEAM[MART83], LDC [BALL84], IRUS [BATE84], and FRED [JAKO86]. CO-OP aims at providing cooperative responses; however, CO-OP lacks a conceptually natural model like the WM of KID. TEAM incorporates a knowledge base similar to the world model; however, TEAM stresses knowledge acquisition[BARR81] issues rather than knowledge base design issues as discussed in this chapter. Like KID, LDC seeks to permit customization by sophisticated users; however, LDC works with loosely structured text files rather than relational databases. IRUS and FRED resemble KID closely in design; they have conceptual database languages to gain DBMS transportability although their data models are different from KID's. The work of Salveter[SALV84] focuses on natural language database update, which KID does not implement currently.

Ideas similar to our method of semantic interpretation using the WM have been pursued by some researchers on natural language understanding, such as Sondheimer et al.[SOND84], and Hayes[HAYE84]. However, Sondheimer et al. do not present general rules using the model like the identification rules in KID. Hayes' parser provides less simple control of the rules than the KID parser in that he uses "multi-strategy" parsing to make the parser robust.

Many of the ideas incorporated in the WM have been adapted from work on semantic data modeling. What is most significant about the WM is that it provides an integrated framework for describing the semantics of a domain of discourse, DB mapping, and linguistic knowledge. The object-oriented features of the WM have been borrowed from LOOPS[BOBR81].

GEM[TSUR84] is similar to our work in that it attempts to implement a semantic data model on a relational DB system. However, GEM's mapping is less flexible than KID's in that GEM restricts implementation of a generalization hierarchy to one relation. EUFID[BURG80] is similar to KID in that it aims to bridge the gap between the English-like input and DB query. However, EUFID's mapping uses an ad hoc representation scheme.

5.6.2 Summary

We explained a knowledge-based approach for designing a portable NLI to DB systems called KID. KID was originally developed for the Japanese language. However, we believe that our framework could be applied to other languages, such as English. KID is an example of applying a semantic data model to NLI design. We believe that our approach to query translation is a practical solution to the problem of implementing semantic data models.

KID is a prototype system, but has been applied to several domains, such as real estate, merchandising, and medical tests. KID has accepted more than 90 percent of the user's requests in each domain. The results of comprehensive evaluation of KID are that the WM is easy to build and KID is very portable.

Chapter 6
HYPERMEDIA APPLICATIONS

This chapter describes an object-oriented database approach to hypermedia applications [ISHI90].

6.1 Introduction

Hypermedia systems such as HyperCard [GOOD87], NoteCard [HALA88], Neptune [DELI86], and Intermedia [YANK88] have a simple data model consisting of nodes and links. They allow flexible access to multimedia data including text, images. Applications of Hypermedia systems vary from personal use such as authoring, idea processing, and information management to CAD and CASE systems [DELI86].

However, application of current hypermedia technology to complex systems such as CAD and CASE systems has several drawbacks stemming from their large-scale data and heterogeneous structures. The drawbacks include lack of abstraction, associative searching facilities, complex object modeling capabilities, support for evolution, programming and database facilities, limited extensibility, and poor performance. Although relational database technology can solve some of these problems, it is weak in modeling and programming. Objected-oriented programming languages [GOLD83][STEF86] can solve complex object modeling, programming, and evolution to some extent, but they lack support for large scale persistent objects which use secondary memory. As a third alternative, an object-oriented DBMS (database management system) [ISHI88] approach can solve more of these problems more elegantly than the above two alternatives because it can integrate an object-oriented programming and database facilities.

We discuss an object-oriented DBMS approach to complex hypermedia applications in this chapter. In Section 6.2, we discuss issues in current hypermedia systems. In Sections 6.3 and 6.4, we describe the model and language of an object-oriented DBMS called *Jasmine* [ISHI88]. In Section 6.5, we explain how Jasmine can be used as a next

105

generation of hypermedia engine to solve these problems. In Section 6.6, we compare our approach with relevant work.

6.2 Current Hypermedia Systems

6.2.1 Common characteristics

Hypermedia systems model domain information by nodes and links. Nodes include multimedia data such as text, images and graphics. They are connected by links. A network consisting of nodes and links represents a hypermedia model.

Hypermedia systems have the following functions in common. First, the user can access hypermedia in an arbitrary order by traversing links attached to nodes. This function is called *nonlinear authoring*. The user can keep track of their access independent of originally defined links. Second, the user can create and modify links freely and attach semantics to them. Third, the user can create and modify nodes freely. Nodes can represent annotations, have multimedia contents, and may contain reference to other nodes. Fourth, the user can access hypermedia in a window-based interface. The user can browse through a node in one window, and most systems allow the user to directly manipulate displayed multimedia data.

6.2.2 Issues

Hypermedia systems used for complex systems such as CAD applications must be able to handle large-scale, heterogeneous structures. The limitations of current systems are:

(1) Current systems lack abstraction mechanisms such as classification [SCHR84] and *generalization* [SMIT77] needed to manage heterogeneous structures. Classification represents types of similar individual nodes. Generalization represents relationships between similar types.

(2) Current systems do not support complex search. Although link-based browsing works well in small homogeneous applications, it is insufficient in scaled-up heterogeneous applications such as CAD. The desired mechanisms include associative searching by flexible combination of conditions on node attributes (links) based on abstraction and *content searching* such as partial string matching. They should allow a *structural search* such as searching by conditions on the number of attribute values and allow partially specified queries on all nodes with particular attributes.

(3) Current systems do not handle creation and manipulation of complex nodes. CAD applications need *complex object* [KIM87] modeling in addition to generalization

and classification. The user wants to operate on a group of nodes as a single entity. The user must be able to browse a complex node in one window. The user must be able to create and destroy complex nodes. Unlike generalization, however, the semantics of complex nodes may vary from one application to another.

We cannot provide the system-defined semantics of complex nodes in advance, so the user must be able to define semantics of nodes dynamically. The user must be able to efficiently store and access complex nodes.

(4) Current systems don't allow the user to add new views to existing hypermedia applications as the applications evolve. In complex applications such as CAD, the user often defines new information by combining items of information rather than defining new items from scratch. The user must be able to define dynamic attributes called *derived attributes* [SHIP81]. Current systems only support static attributes.

(5) Current systems cannot support a full programming facility. Complex applications need searching and manipulation of nodes by use of programs. Current systems cannot allow the user to compactly specify such programs. The user must be able to specify actions to be triggered when certain events occur. We must provide a general-purpose programming language in which a whole application system can be programmed. High performance is also required.

(6) Most current systems provide no support for keeping track of *versions*. Only Neptune [DELI87] can support version histories. CAD applications need to manage versions of design objects. They must also be able to represent design alternatives in contrast to simple versions. A sophisticated version mechanism to integrate these concepts must thus be provided.

(7) Current systems cannot provide *database amenities* such as multi-user support, transaction recovery, and high performance. A group of users must be able to securely design an artifact cooperatively in LAN-based workstations. Query optimization for complex queries must be provided.

(8) More extensibility is required. The user must be able to flexibly add new attributes, operations, and media types to existing systems. The user must thus be allowed to extend the functions of existing systems with as little effort as possible and to interactively modify and execute these systems. HyperCard [GOOD87] allows high extensibility with Hypertalk. The number of attributes and the amount of data must be unlimited.

The next generation of hypermedia systems is expected to solve these problems. Extending current hypermedia systems makes them less flexible. A layered architecture is more flexible. Relational databases seem promising for this purpose. However, the current database technology has drawbacks in complex object modeling and programming facilities. Another candidate, object-oriented programming language technology, is good at modeling and programming but it has performance problems for handling large-scale persistent objects. It is difficult for developers of hypermedia systems to combine these two concepts. Therefore, an object-oriented DBMS approach integrating database and object-oriented programming language facilities is required. The system we developed, Jasmine [ISHI88], is promising in that respect. The following two sections give an outline of Jasmine, comparing Jasmine with current *object-oriented database systems*(OODBS) [AGRA89] [BANE87] [LECL89] [LYNG87] [MAIE86].

6.3 Data   Model

We summarize the semantics of our object-oriented data model, focusing on its features relevant to hypermedia applications.

6.3.1 Object semantics

We describe structural semantics of objects which are an integration of a functional data model [SHIP81] and *frames* [MINS75] in AI. Objects are a collection of attributes, which directly represent structural and behavioral knowledge of a domain. Attributes are categorized into *enumerated attributes* and *procedural attributes*. Enumerated attributes are used to represent structural knowledge such as Name and Doctor. Procedural attributes are used to represent behavioral knowledge (programs) such as make-certificate. Enumerated and procedural attributes can be uniformly treated in our manipulation language. Objects are categorized into *instances* denoting individual knowledge, or factual knowledge, and *classes* defining attributes applicable to similar instances, or generic knowledge.

We define attributes based on functions in a functional data model. An attribute is a mapping from a set of objects to a set of objects. In general, the attribute takes a set of objects as input and gives a set of objects as output. In particular, if the attribute returns a set of one element (*singleton set*), it is viewed as returning an object rather than a set. An attribute which always returns a singleton set is called a *singleton-valued attribute*. An attribute which possibly returns a set of objects, not a singleton, is called a *multiple-valued attribute*. The set in our context is a *bag* [SHIP81], a set which allows duplicates of objects.

Objects are identified by an *object identifier* (OID). An OID is generated by the system and represented by the system-defined attribute Oid which the user can reference. An object with an OID is called a *reference object*. In contrast, string and number objects have only values, no OID. Such objects are called *immediate objects*.

A class defines attributes applicable to its instances, like a type in a programming language. Attributes consist of facets [MINS75] which denote functional annotation of the attribute and differentiate our object model from other functional data models [SHIP81] [LYNG87]. Consider the class PATIENT as an example (See Figure 6.1). The keyword *Enumerated* is followed by the definition of user-supplied enumerated attributes. The *name* facet such as Doctor denotes the name of an attribute. The *class* facet before the name facet denotes the function range class such as FLOAT before Height. The value of the attribute of an instance must be an instance of the range class (See Figure 6.2). The functional domain of the attribute is the class being defined, PATIENT. The *multiple* facet denotes that the attribute is a multiple-valued function such as Temperature. The *mandatory* facet denotes that the attribute allows no null value such as Doctor and Weight (total function). The mandatory attribute, an attribute which is specified mandatory facet, must have its value specified at the time of instantiation. The *default* facet contains a default value referenced when the attribute value is not yet specified such as Category of PATIENT.

```
PATIENT
    Db              MEDICAL
    Super           PERSON
    Enumerated      DOCTOR          Doctor    mandatory
                    STRING          Category           default "outpatient"
                    INTEGER         Cardinality        common
                    FLOAT Temperature        multiple
                            constraint {(value > 34.0 && value <43.0)}
                    FLOAT Weight    mandatory constraint {(value > 0.0)}
                    FLOAT Height    constraint {(value > 0.0)  If-needed
                                                  { int h;
                                                  h = self.Weight;
                                                  return h + 100.0;}
    Procedural      CERTIFICATE    make-certificate (date)
                    STRING date;
                    { CERTIFICATE c;
                    int i;
                    c = <CERTIFICATE>.instantiate ();
                    c.Patientname = self.Name;
                    c.Doctorname = self.Doctor.Name;
                    c.Diseasename = self.Disease.name;
                    c.Date = date;
                    . . .
                    return c;}
```

Figure 6.1. Example of class definition.

MedicalPatient007
    Sex   "male"
    Age   36
    Name   "James Bond"
    Address   "Tokyo"
    Doctor   MedicalDoctor010
    Category   "inpatient"
    Temperature   36.5 37.3 38.1
    Weight   76.0
    Height   181.0

Figure 6.2. Example of an instance.

The behavioral knowledge can also be attached to the enumerated attribute unlike other OODBS. The knowledge represented by the demon facets is invoked by different triggers. The procedure in the *constraint* facet, the constraint demon, is invoked before a value is inserted to the attribute. The value is set to the attribute only if the procedure returns true. Constraint demons such as Temperature can allow the user to specify complex and general constraints. The *if-added* demon is invoked after the value is inserted to the attribute. The *if-needed* demon, invoked if the referenced attribute has a null value, computes a value such as Height of PATIENT. The user can combine these demons to implement active databases [MORG83].

The keyword *Procedural* is followed by the definition of user-supplied procedural attributes. Procedural attributes such as make-medical-certificate also have facets. The class facet denotes the range class of the procedural function. In particular, if the procedural attribute returns a null value, system-defined VOID is specified as the range class. The procedural attribute can take parameters such as date, in addition to the domain object. Procedural attributes can have *before* and *after* demons which are invoked before and after the main function.

Notice that only the attribute name needs to be unique in a class. Different classes may have attributes of the same name with the same purpose but with different implementations. At invocation, an appropriate implementation is chosen depending on the class type. This mechanism called *polymorphism* [STEF86] is unambiguous, thus eliminating the need for the concept of a *role* [SHIP81][LYNG87].

6.3.2 Classification and generalization

In this subsection we describe object semantics associated with *classification* [SCHR84] and *generalization* [SMIT77].

A class is not only a type defining characteristics common to its instances but is also viewed as a set of instances. PERSON is a set of persons (See Figure 6.3). Our concept of class directly represents classification. This eliminates the need for extra concepts and simplifies the object manipulation language design. Unlike Jasmine, Smalltalk-80 [GOLD83]-based systems such as GemStone [MAIE86] introduce a *collection* in addition to a class.

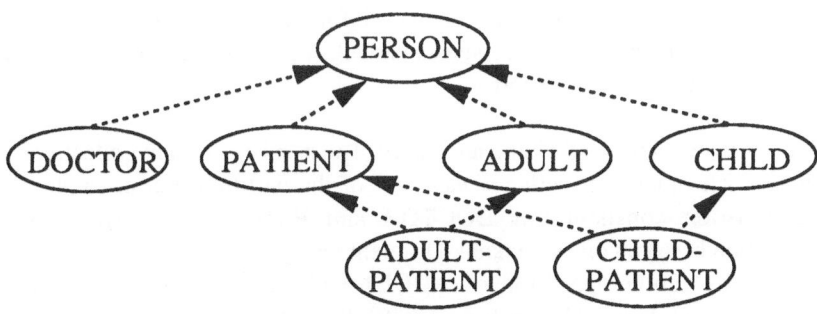

Figure 6.3. Example of a class lattice.

An instance belongs to only one class intrinsically. The class is called an *intrinsic class*; its instances are called *intrinsic instances*. If the user creates an instance from a class such as PATIENT by the system-defined procedural attribute instantiate, the instance is an intrinsic instance of the class PATIENT. The intrinsic class is denoted by the system-defined attribute Class. It is similar to a *most specialized class* of TAXIS [NIXO87]. Consider an alternative which allows one instance to belong to more than one class. This alternative doesn't enable one class to provide full information of the whole instance. It is inappropriate for *model-based processing* [ISHI87] in AI which is mainly based on generic knowledge or classes. The alternative makes an object model less understandable and makes maintenance related to instance modification more complex.

The system-defined attribute Super supports generalization. The superclass, for example, PERSON, includes its subclasses, PATIENT, as a set. Instances of a subclass belong to the superclass virtually but not intrinsically. The interpretation of a class is the set union of the intrinsic instances of the class and the instances of its subclasses. A leaf class has only intrinsic instances. The characteristics which hold in the superclass hold in the subclass. Thus, the attributes of the superclass are inherited by the subclass, such as Age of PATIENT. An attribute can be newly defined in the subclass such as Doctor of PATIENT.

Any class in a generalization hierarchy can have its intrinsic instances. In particular, intrinsic instances of a nonleaf class can represent *incomplete knowledge* of the domain. For example, PERSON intrinsic instances directly denote a set of persons known to be neither a patient nor a doctor. Intrinsic instances can model the domain knowledge as it is. This differentiates the Jasmine model from other models. The instance may be specialized to a more specific class if new information is added in the future. For example, a person who gets ill becomes a patient. An instance can move around classes in a hierarchy as the database evolves.

A class is divided into disjoint subclasses. Those subclasses are collectively called a *partition*. Each subclass is called a *member* of the partition. For example, PERSON has a partition consisting of DOCTOR and PATIENT. A partition denotes a categorization based on one viewpoint. Different viewpoints generate different partitions. PERSON has another partition of ADULT and CHILD. Members of distinctive partitions may not be disjoint such as PATIENT and ADULT. *Categorization conditions* can be explicitly specified to make the partition semantics clear such as "Age >= 18" of ADULT unlike other OODBS such as O2 [LECL89]. Then the attribute Age is called a *categorization attribute*.

Our semantics allow a class to have *multiple-superclasses*. They must be nondisjoint members of different partitions of a class since a subclass with multiple-superclasses is included by all of the superclasses. The attribute Super introduces a lattice, not a strict hierarchy. The Super semantics also holds to multiple-superclasses. For example, ADULT-PATIENT inherits Doctor from PATIENT and Occupation from ADULT (*multiple-inheritance*). Instances of ADULT-PATIENT can belong to both PATIENT and ADULT virtually.

A class is an instance of the system-defined class CLASS because we want to be able to operate on classes and instances uniformly. Unlike TAXIS, we don't introduce *metaclasses* making the object model more complex.

6.4 Database Programming Language

We briefly describe a database programming language called *Jasmine/C* needed by the development of hypermedia applications.

6.4.1 Object expressions

The basic unit of set-oriented access is an *object expression*, which consists of a class name optionally followed by a series of one or more attribute names:

class
class.attribute-1.attribute-2 ...attribute-n

The object expression *class* denotes a set of instance objects according to the class semantics. The expression *class.attribute-1* denotes a set of instance objects as the attribute value. In general, the object expression evaluates to a set of objects as the values of the last attribute. As attributes are functions, the object expression corresponds to a functional composition which denotes a *functional join* or *implicit join* [ZANI83] by traversing attributes representing relationships between objects and eliminates the need for join predicates in most queries, like the *dot-notation* of GEM [ZANI83]. The object expression allows the user to directly access components of complex objects (*structural access*) unlike other C-based systems such as ODE [AGRA89], O2 [LECL89].

Inherited attributes such as PATIENT.Age and newly-defined attributes such as PATIENT.Height are treated in a uniform fashion. Multiple-valued attributes such as PATIENT.Temperature and singlet-valued attributes such as PATIENT.Weight can be specified uniformly. The multiple values are normalized into a flat set of objects.The enumerated and procedural attributes are treated in the same way to both retrieve and manipulate objects associatively. The system-defined and user-defined attributes are uniformly treated to ease customization of the language. The uniformity described above leads to compact specification of the language Jasmine/C.

6.4.2 Queries

A set-oriented access query has the following form:

<target part> where <condition part>

The target part usually consists of an object expression although the target part can take a list of object expressions. The condition part consists of a logical combination of simple conditions which compare object expressions with comparison operators such as ==, !=, >, >=, <, and <=. The query form evaluates to a set of the target objects (OIDs or values) satisfying the condition. For example, to find all the names of doctors who work in the pediatrics department and are in charge of patients over 13 years of age, the user forms a query as follows:

> PATIENT.Doctor.Name
>> where PATIENT.Doctor.Dept == "pediatrics" and PATIENT.Age > 13

Immediate objects are compared by ==, !=, >, >=, <, and <=, based on values. Reference objects are compared by == and != based on OIDs. These two operators correspond to the *is* operator of GEM [ZANI83] and *isnot* operator of EXODUS [CARE88]. Assume Disease and Specialty are reference attributes (See Figure 6.4):

> DOCTOR.Name where PATIENT.Name == "James Bond"
>> and PATIENT.Disease == DOCTOR.Specialty

This query finds the name of a doctor who specializes in James' disease. In general, joins are classified into implicit and explicit joins.

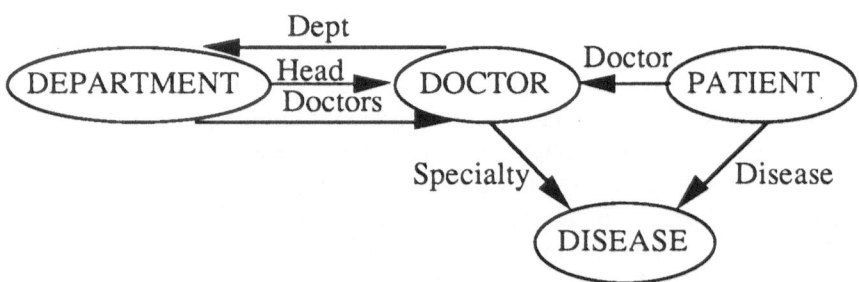

Figure 6.4. Part of a medical database structure.

Jasmine can also support explicit joins as follows:

> PATIENT where PATIENT.Age > PATIENT.Doctor.Age

Comparison of multiple-valued attributes is interpreted as *at least one* value satisfying the condition. The following query retrieves patients who ran a temperature of higher than 37.0 degrees centigrade at least once.

PATIENT where PATIENT.Temperature > 37.0

The Jasmine classes eliminate the need for *collection* classes and *select* messages of GemStone [MAIE86]. Declaration of loop variables is unnecessary unlike ODE [AGRA89]. The user can specify a query more compactly.

6.4.3 Incomplete knowledge access

Any class, leaf or nonleaf, in a generalization lattice can be specified in a set-oriented query. According to the interpretation of a class, the intrinsic instances of a nonleaf class and the instances of its subclasses can be retrieved at the same time. For example, to find persons who are older than forty:

PERSON where PERSON.Age > 40

This causes a query be specified compactly because several queries against subclasses such as PATIENT and DOCTOR can be formulated in a single query.

The user can retrieve objects without precise specification. A general class can be specified in a query together with an attribute defined in its subclasses. Then the general class is automatically specialized to the subclasses. For example, to find the names of persons who work in the surgery department:

PERSON.Name where PERSON.Dept.Name == "surgery"

The class PERSON is automatically specialized to the subclass DOCTOR with the attribute Dept defined. In the extreme case, OBJECT can be used in a query. This mechanism fits with how we define some concepts by differentiating a general concept by providing specializing attributes. The user can thus formulate a query without knowing specificity like a natural language query.

The user can impose a condition on the categorization attribute of a general class with a partition. If the specified condition matches with some of the categorization conditions of the partition, the specified class can be specialized to some of the partition members. For example, to find persons who are younger than thirteen:

PERSON where PERSON.Age < 13

The class PERSON is automatically specialized to CHILD. Thus, the query is transformed to a more efficient one. Other OODBS such as O2 [LECL89] lack this ability to flexibly access incomplete knowledge.

6.4.4 Set-oriented operation

A set-oriented query is not restricted to only retrieval. The user can do operations other than retrieval in the set-oriented access by using procedural attributes, which can be specified in any part of an attribute of an object expression of a query. The additional parameters of the procedural attribute are given in parentheses:

> *class.attr.procedural-attribute(parm1, parm2)*

To make a copy of serious patients' medical certificates dated January 8, 1989, the user formulates the query:

> PATIENT.make-medical-certificate("19890108")
>   where PATIENT.Condition == "serious"

Assuming that we operate on objects set-theoretically in other systems such as ODE [AGRA89] and O2 [LECL89], we then have to retrieve a set of objects and scan and operate on each object in an iteration construct. In contrast, Jasmine makes this type of iteration implicit and allows the user to compactly specify a query without knowing the details. This increases productivity in application development.

Of course, we can also specify procedural attributes in incomplete knowledge access. If we specify a general class whose subclasses have procedural attributes of the same name which have different implementations, the different attributes are invoked in a single query at the same time. For example, to display heterogeneous media objects such as images, graphics, created January 8, 1989 at the same time, the user specifies the following query:

> MEDIA.display() where MEDIA.Date == "19890108"

We can specify the system-defined and user-defined procedural attributes in the same way unlike ODE [AGRA89]. The user can print interns who work in the surgery department by use of the system-defined print:

> DOCTOR.print( ) where DOCTOR.Dept.Name == "surgery"
>   and DOCTOR.Status == "internship"

The system-defined attributes include object modification operations such as *put*, *delete*. They can be invoked in a set-oriented query. The following query sets James' temperature to 36.5 degrees centigrade.

> PATIENT.put("Temperature", 36.5) where PATIENT.Name == "James Bond"

Because we make no distinction between the system-defined and user-defined attributes in a query, the user can customize Jasmine/C without changing the language processor. The user can extend the functions of Jasmine/C just by adding the user-defined procedural attributes unlike other OODBS.

6.4.5 Procedural attributes in conditions

Procedural attributes can also be specified in object expressions in the condition part of a query unlike other OODBS such as O2. They are used to filter objects procedurally. A content-based search of multimedia data can be done by defining a dedicated attribute as follows:

PATIENT where PATIENT.Xray.like(sample-1) == true

This finds a patient whose X-ray looks like sample-1 containing some disease.

Procedural attributes both in the target part and in the condition part are compiled to directly access objects in database buffers. This eliminates the need for transferring unnecessary data from the buffer to application programs and executes the application programs more efficiently than conventional approaches.

6.4.6 Demons

If demons, such as if-added and if-needed, are attached to attributes specified in object expressions of a query, they are invoked by associated events such as if-added and if-needed. The events are triggered by the invocation of procedural attributes such as put and the reference of enumerated attributes such as Height. The actions invoked after events happen, such as the if-added demon of Condition of PATIENT, are defined like a procedural attribute. This mechanism is used for developing active databases containing triggers and alerters. ODE [AGRA89] also supports active databases, but not by demons. For example,

PATIENT.put("Condition", "serious") where PATIENT.Name == "James Bond"

This query invokes the action of giving a notice to the head of the department of James' doctor that James' condition has gotten serious.

6.4.7 Class operations

A class is modeled by the system-defined class CLASS. Classes can be associatively retrieved like instances:

CLASS.print() where CLASS.Enumerated.Class == <DOCTOR>

The above query prints classes which have DOCTOR as enumerated attributes. This helps greatly as a *data dictionary* when the user makes a query. It is also important when the user defines a new class by modifying existent classes. For example, the user of a CAD system retrieves a library of design solutions represented by classes and modifies these designs to satisfy the given specifications. Other OODBS such as ODE [AGRA89] lack this ability to flexibly manipulate generic knowledge.

6.5 Application OF JASMINE

6.5.1 Hypermedia engine

We can use a general-purpose DBMS Jasmine as a hypermedia engine so that the user can flexibly build hypermedia systems. Jasmine provides the basic functions needed for a hypermedia engine as system-defined classes (See Figure 6.5).

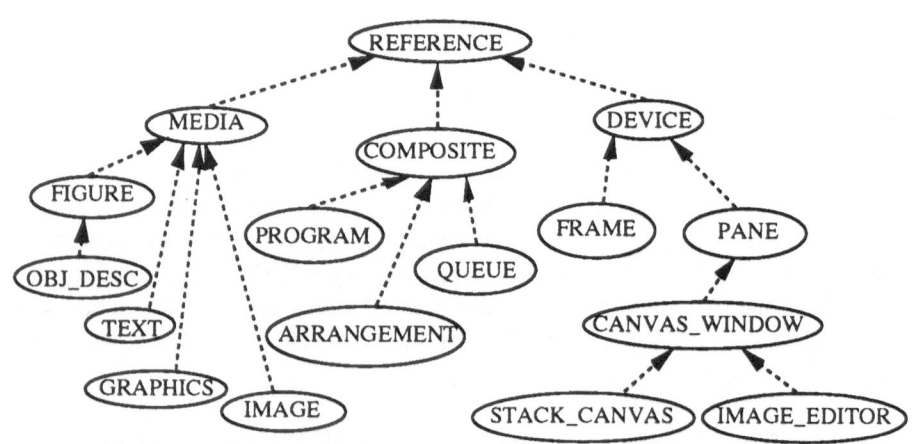

Figure 6.5. Part of system-defined classes.

The user can define basic node types by using MEDIA classes. They include TEXT, GRAPHICS, and IMAGE. MEDIA objects have primitive objects stored in secondary memory. GRAPHICS has primitives such as polygons. TEXT has source texts.

IMAGE has RGB pixel data. Media data to be displayed is converted from these primitive attributes by if-needed demons when it is displayed for the first time. MEDIA objects have the same interface or polymorphic procedural attribute such as display, move, and change-size. They can be uniformly treated independent of media types. WINDOW objects can display MEDIA objects. FRAME, a subclass of WINDOW, consists of multiple PANEs. IMAGE_EDITOR can read image data from the scanner and make it an object.

Nodes represented as complex objects can be displayed in one window. A FIGURE object has multiple ARRANGEMENT objects which keep displayed media objects and their locations. In particular, OBJ_DESC objects are used to display formatted descriptions of objects. Displayed objects can be accessed in a direct manipulation interface. This can be elegantly attained by an object-oriented approach. For example, consider a map containing scenic spots. The FIGURE and ARRANGEMENT objects of the map manage scenic spot objects and their locations.

If the user points to a displayed object by clicking, the system uses the procedural attribute of FIGURE to search an object whose display area contains the clicked point. And the user can operate on the pointed object by specifying its procedural attributes. Objects contained by texts can also be directly accessed.

Both a set-oriented query and direct manipulation are managed by STACK_CANVAS windows. The result consisting of one or more objects is managed by QUEUE objects. This can keep trails of user access of hypermedia objects. The user can walk through the trails by invoking the next and last procedural attributes for QUEUE and the push and pop for STACK_CANVAS.

6.5.2 Hypermedia model

We describe how hypermedia is modeled by using Jasmine. Consider sightseeing in Kyoto as an example. Nodes and links can be modeled by objects and attributes. We define SCENICSPOT and LIBRARY node types as subclasses of the system-defined COMPOSITE class (See Figure 6.6). Links between GUIDEBOOK and SECTION nodes can be represented by attributes. Different types of links correspond to different attributes. Media types are represented by TEXT, GRAPHICS, and IMAGE classes. The attribute Appearance of SCENICSPOT is IMAGE, and Paragraph of SECTION is TEXT. Annotations can be also represented by attributes such as Scenicspot of SECTION. The user can define an arbitrary number of attributes in objects. The size of data such as image is not limited.

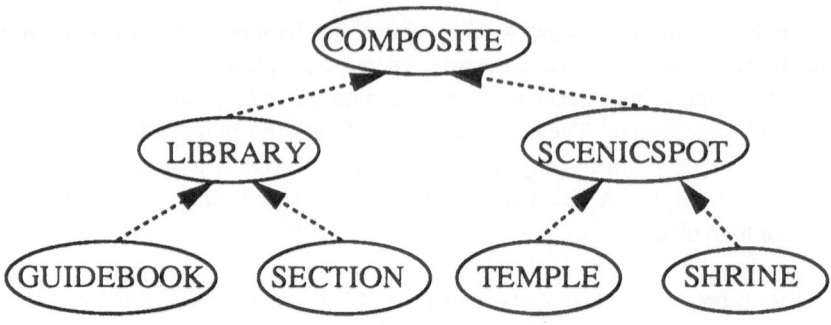

Figure 6.6. Part of node classes for Kyoto sightseeing.

Similar node classes are organized into a lattice by Super. TEMPLE and SHRINE can inherit attribute definitions from their superclass SCENICSPOT through Super. The user can cluster relevant heterogeneous node classes into one *database* to establish partitioning, and one or more databases in an application can be used at the same time. Note that large-scale, persistent objects in a database can be used without knowing whether they are resident in main memory [ISHI88].

6.5.3 Solutions

We describe solutions to the remaining issues addressed in Section 6.2.

(1) In addition to direct manipulation, Jasmine enables the user to retrieve node objects associatively by specifying complex search conditions, including procedural attributes and logical operators. The associative search is based on classification (Class) and generalization (Super). Content searching can be done by using procedural attributes such as contains. For example, the user can retrieve the Section of a GUIDEBOOK node whose paragraph has an author named Ishikawa and begins with the string "This" as follows:

> GUIDEBOOK.Section
>> where GUIDEBOOK.Section.Paragraph.contains("This$") == true
>> and SECTION.Author == "Ishikawa"

Structural searching can be done. The following query retrieves node objects which have a particular attribute Author with exactly two values by using a procedural attribute count:

> OBJECT where OBJECT.Author.count() == 2

Then the system executes the query after automatically specializing OBJECT into SECTION which has the attribute Author. The user can thus retrieve generic nodes efficiently without knowing the specific names of node classes. Multiple node classes can be retrieved at the same time by specifying a nonleaf class in a lattice:

SCENICSPOT where SCENICSPOT.Area == "east"

This retrieves all TEMPLE and SHRINE node objects located in the east area. The user can retrieve only generic nodes by specifying conditions on the attribute Class.

For example, the following query retrieves scenic spots other than temples and shrines:

SCENICSPOT where SCENICSPOT.Class == <SCENICSPOT>

(2) A Part relationship induced by complex object nodes means some constraints among a complex object and its component objects. The semantics of Part is not always the same in all attributes unlike that of Super. So the system cannot provide the semantics in advance. Instead, Jasmine can allow the user to define his own semantics of Part by using demons which are triggered when associated events occur. Consider a Part relationship between GUIDEBOOK and SECTION. If we use the hypothetical attribute Life, the following constraint means that only while a complex object is present, its component objects can be present.

GUIDEBOOK.Life contains GUIDEBOOK.SECTION.Life temporally

This constraint can be defined as before and after demons of procedural attributes instantiate and destroy of GUIDEBOOK as follows:

Procedural VOID instantiate after
  { self.Section.instantiate() }

Procedural VOID destroy before
  { self.Section.destroy() }

These attributes guarantee that the SECTION nodes are automatically created just after the GUIDEBOOK nodes are and that the SECTION nodes are automatically destroyed just before the GUIDEBOOK nodes are. Next consider the attribute Numberofchar contained by GUIDEBOOK objects. The following constraint holds:

GUIDEBOOK.Numberofchar = sum of GUIDEBOOK.Section.Numberofchar

This constraint is defined by using an if-needed demon of Numberofchar as follows:

Enumerated INTEGER Numberofchar if-needed
{ self.Section.Numberofchar.sum() }

In case of display, the following constraint holds:

GUIDEBOOK.Displayarea contains GUIDEBOOK.Section.Displayarea spatially

This is defined as a before demon of an attribute display as follows:

Procedural VOID display before
{ self.Section.display(window) }

Like these, constraints associated with Part can be expressed by demons. Note that a complex object and its component objects can have the same interface such as display by polymorphism and can be treated uniformly. Complex object nodes represented as a subclass of the system-defined class RELATION can be stored in nested relations [ROTH88] and be efficiently accessed without joins.

(3) Jasmine allows the user to derive new views of a hypermedia model by using procedural attributes. Procedural attributes can define new attributes by combining existing enumerated (static) and procedural (dynamic) attributes as follows:

Procedural BOOLEAN createdWithin3DaysNotByMe ()
{ self.CreatedDate.within(Today, 3) == true
  and self.Creator != Userid }

This attribute can define virtual nodes [HALA88] which were created within three days by a person other than the user:

OBJECT where OBJECT.createdWithin3DaysNotByMe () == true

Virtual links [HALA88] can be defined for SCENICSPOT as follows:

Procedural SCENICSPOT neighborhood () multiple
{ SCENICSPOT where SCENICSPOT.within(self, 3) == true }

This can be used to retrieve neighboring (i.e., within three kilometers) scenic spots of a specified scenic spot (e.g., the Heian Shrine):

SHRINE.neighborhood () where SHRINE.Name == "the Heian Shrine"

(4) Jasmine allows the user to retrieve and manipulate objects by using procedures.

This can be attained by enabling the user to specify procedural attributes in the target and condition parts of an associative query. The following query retrieves temples within four kilometers from here by using a procedural attribute within:

TEMPLE where TEMPLE.within(Here, 4) == true

The following query computes the total fee of recommended temples by using a procedural attribute sum:

TEMPLE.Fee.sum() where TEMPLE.Rank == "recommended"

The user defines procedural attributes such as within of SCENICSPOT by programming them in Jasmine/C as follows:

```
Procedural BOOLEAN within (source, distance)
        SCENICSPOT source;
        INTEGER distance, diffx, diffy;
        { diffx = self.LocationX-source.LocationX;
          diffy = self.LoactionY-source.LocationY;
          return diffx*diffx+diffy*diffy < distance*distance; }
```

Procedural attributes are compiled and efficiently executed. At compilation, inherited attributes are searched and statically bound to reduce overhead of dynamic searching done by conventional object-oriented programming languages.

Procedural attributes, demons, and a whole application using hypermedia can be programmed in Jasmine/C. In general, programs in Jasmine can be modeled by the system-defined class PROGRAM, which has enumerated attributes such as source, binary, and procedural attributes such as compile and link. Program objects can be retrieved associatively and compiled dynamically. For example, the following query compiles programs created on May 5, 1989:

PROGRAM.compile() where PROGRAM.CreatedDate == "19890505"

(5) Jasmine databases not only establish disjoint partitioning but also overlapping structures. The user can use different databases to contain alternative configurations of an original hypermedia model. Because of this feature, a database can serve several purposes.

First, we can use a database to provide a versioning mechanism. A distinction is made between versions and design alternatives of a design object. Versions are created because of bug fixes and releases. Design alternatives are created to explore different implementations. Design alternatives are used concurrently while versions emphasize historical orders. We can make versions (e.g., a revised edition of a GUIDEBOOK) by freezing a database comprising a snapshot of a hypermedia model. We can explore design alternatives (e.g., alternative configurations of SECTION structures) by switching among multiple databases.

Second, Jasmine databases can be used to establish a cooperative environment where each user of a project can work together in his private context generated by modifying a public hypermedia model. Consider a situation where teams of authors write a single guidebook. If we partition an application into a project database (e.g., containing a whole GUIDEBOOK node which teams of authors share) and private databases (e.g., containing only portions of SECTION nodes of which an author takes care), we can make a private workspace by combining and merging private and project databases. Like these, our databases work the same way as *web* of Intermedia [YANK88] and *context* of Neptune [DELI87].

(6) Database features such as multi-user access and transaction management are supported by system-defined classes. The class DB has enumerated attributes such as Lock and Log, and procedural attributes such as open, close, and destroy for database management. The class SYSTEM has enumerated attributes such Nobuf, Nodb, Transaction and procedural attributes such as open, close, begintransaction, endtransaction, and restoretransaction. A typical database session is represented by combining these procedural attributes.

Design transactions (e.g., editing SECTION nodes) may take from several hours to days. When the user makes some mistakes during a design transaction, simple abortion of the whole transaction is inadequate because it also loses other valuable modifications. In Jasmine, we represent such a design transaction as a collection of usual transactions which are defined by transaction operations described above. The user can undo the operation causing mistakes by executing another transaction which compensates the operation.

Change notification [HALA88] associated with collaborative work can be achieved by using demons. The following demon is triggered by the action of changing the fee of a scenic spot:

        Enumerated INTEGER Fee if-updated
            { notify(self.Section.Author, value) }

This then notifies the author of an associated Section that the fee of a scenic spot has been changed.

Jasmine generates optimized codes for object access [ISHI88]. For example, joins generated by object expressions in a query can be efficiently executed by using indexing and hashing [YAMA89]. Links between node objects in main memory are represented by pointers to efficiently process link traversal.

(7) The user can easily add new static and dynamic attributes by using inheritance supported by Super. Polymorphic attributes of new node classes (e.g., move of 3-D ANIMATION) can be added without affecting attributes of existing node classes (e.g., move of IMAGE). The user can extend the functionality of the language of hypermedia systems just by defining procedural attributes because the system makes no distinction between user-defined attributes such as neighborhood and system-defined attributes such as put. These can be aided by our database programming language Jasmine/C. We provide a language interpreter to enable the user to interactively run a modified system after adding new functions.

6.6 Conclusion

6.6.1 Related work

This work has been inspired by Halasz's work [HALA88] which discusses issues of current hypermedia systems. Our approach to hypermedia is similar to Neptune [DELI86], Intermedia [YANK88], and Shadow [CARA89]. Neptune is built on top of HAM, a hypermedia engine; however, HAM has only a bit stream interface, that is, no interpretation of media contents is done while Jasmine provides basic functions for media objects. Neptune focuses more on version control and context support. Intermedia tries to extend its functionality by using an object-oriented DBMS called Encore [SMIT87] like our work. However, Encore does not provide an object-oriented programming language as Jasmine does. The integration of Intermedia with Encore is less seamless than that of our approach. Shadow is implemented in Strobe, an object-oriented programming language that supports programming and object storage. However, Shadow cannot allow efficient retrieval of large-scale data. In our opinion, Jasmine supports more advanced functionality as a hypermedia engine than HAM, Encore, and Strobe do.

6.6.2 Experiment

We developed a prototype hypermedia system which serves as a guide for Kyoto. This allows associative retrieval of node objects such as temples and bookguides. Procedural attributes such as sum and within can be specified in target and condition parts of a query to retrieve and manipulate nodes procedurally. We can access virtual links such as neighborhood. In one window we can display and manipulate complex object nodes such as maps. Objects contained by texts can be directly accessed to display (See Figure 6.7). Nonleaf nodes such as scenic spots can be retrieved. The whole application is programmed in Jasmine/C and managed as a separate database. This prototype has confirmed the feasibility of Jasmine as a next generation of hypermedia engine.

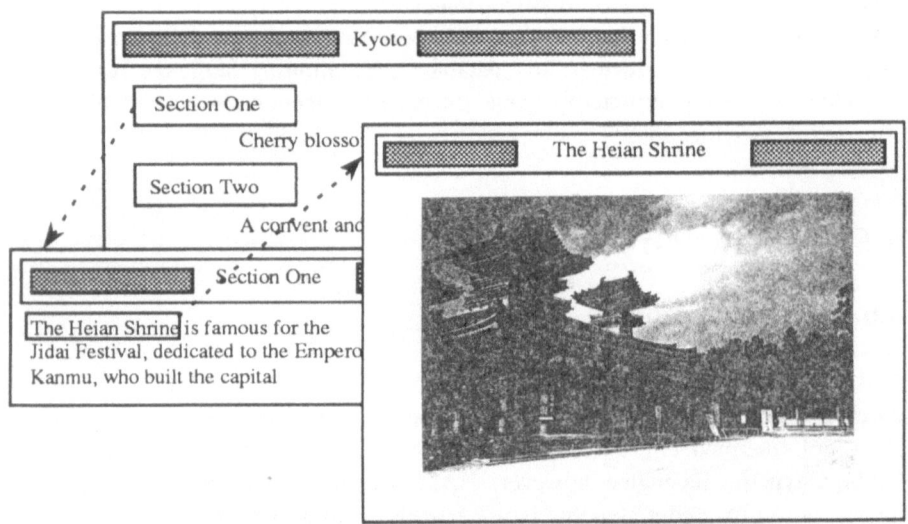

Figure 6.7. Example of displayed nodes.

Chapter 7
ENGINEERING APPLICATIONS

This chapter describes an object-oriented database approach to engineering applications [ISHI91a].

7.1 Introduction

Complex, large-scale applications such as CAD and hypermedia require advanced databases. We take CAD applications as an example. Conventional drawing-oriented CAD systems do not sufficiently improve the total productivity and reliability of engineering tasks. To this end, we wish to provide support for engineering processes other than drawing and manage not only primary design data but also associated engineering information. We use databases as a software platform to attain these goals. Relational databases are appropriate for business applications, but inappropriate for complex, large-scale engineering tasks due to their fixed data model. Instead, *object-oriented databases* (OODBs) [MAIE86] [ISHI93a] [DEUX90] [KIM90] are expected to be the next-generation of databases. In Section 7.2, we briefly describe the functionality and implementation of an OODB system called *Jasmine*. In Section 7.3, we discuss design data management, intelligent CAD support, and engineering information management as requirements for support of engineering tasks. In Section 7.4, 7.5, and 7.6, we explain our OODB solutions to the above requirements, which are embodied in a prototype intelligent CAD system, called *HyperCAD* [ISHI91a].

7.2 Object-Oriented Database

We will briefly describe Jasmine [ISHI93a], focusing on its features relevant to engineering applications.

7.2.1 Functionality

First, we describe the object model of Jasmine. Objects consist of a collection of *attributes*, which are categorized into *enumerated attributes (properties)* and *procedural attributes (methods)*. Properties denote object structures and methods denote operations on objects. Objects are categorized into *instances* and *classes*. Instances denote individual data and classes denote types (i.e., structures) and operations applicable to instances of the class. Instances consist of a collection of attribute names and values. Classes consist of attribute names and definitions, and associated information such as demons. Objects are identified by values of the system-defined attribute *object identifier* (OID). Therefore, objects with the same object identifier in a consistent database have the same values. On the other hand, values such as numbers and character strings have no OIDs but do have classes defined by the system. Objects with OIDs are called *reference objects* and values with no OIDs *immediate objects*. Objects can have other objects (i.e., OIDs) as attribute values. This enables the user to directly define *complex objects (composite objects)* [KIM90].

Classes are organized into a hierarchy (more strictly, a lattice) along *generalization* relationships. This hierarchy is called a *class hierarchy*. A superclass in a class hierarchy is denoted by the system-defined attribute *Super*. Classes (i.e., *subclasses*) can inherit attribute definitions from their superclasses. The user can make instances (i.e., *instantiate*) from any class in a class hierarchy unlike Smalltalk-80 [GOLD83]. Such instances are called *intrinsic instances* of the class.

Classes not only define object types and methods, but they are also interpreted as a set of instances. That is, the instances of a class is the union of intrinsic instances of the class and all its subclasses. This differentiates Jasmine from other OODBs such as GemStone [MAIE86] where the user must define separate classes both as type and as set. Objects can have a set of objects as well as a singleton object as attribute values. The former are called *multiple-valued attributes* and the latter *singleton-valued attributes*.

The user can attach demons to attributes. *Constraint demons* are checked before insertion of values into attributes and only if they return true, the values are actually inserted. *If-needed, if-added, if-removed,* and *if-updated demons* are invoked at reference, insertion, deletion, and replacement of values. *Before* and *after demons* are invoked before and after the methods they are attached to are invoked. The user can combine these demons to flexibly implement *active databases* [MORG83].

In Jasmine, the user manipulates objects by sending messages to objects just as in object-oriented programming languages. This type of access is called *singleton access*. The user can assign values to attributes and reference attribute values. Jasmine allows *set-oriented access* in addition to singleton access. Set-oriented access is done by a query on objects. The basic unit of an object query is an *object expression*, a class name followed by a series of attribute names with "." between. Object expressions eliminate the need for most of equijoin predicates in relational databases. The user can also specify methods in object expressions. An object query consists of target and condition parts. The target part is a list of object expressions. The condition part is a logical combination of simple conditions comparing object expressions by comparison operators.

The user can combine singleton-access and set-oriented access to make application programs. An element of a set of objects is assigned to *object variables* and is manipulated by sending messages to the object variables.The introduction of object variables reduces *impedance mismatch* between a programming language and a database language [MAIE86]. As the user can specify object queries as well as simple manipulation of attributes in methods, the user can define virtual objects by using such methods as described later. A query on superclasses returns all the instances of the class and its subclasses, so the user can retrieve by a single Jasmine query what would take multiple relational database queries to retrieve. By specifying methods in a query, the user can retrieve and manipulate objects in a set-oriented manner. If a superclass is specified with a method in a query, methods dedicated to instances of the class and its subclasses can be invoked simultaneously. That is, *polymorphism* [STEF86] can be facilitated in a set-oriented manner. A query can also make new instances from more than one class like joins in a relational database.

Application programs written by Jasmine are precompiled into C programs. During this process, references to attributes are statically resolved to reduce the burden of dynamic search, so the C programs can execute efficiently. A set-oriented query can also be interpreted interactively. Objects are basically persistent in that they exist over program execution, though the user can make temporary objects which exist only during program execution like a conventional programming language. A Jasmine database usually consists of several classes. The user can use several databases concurrently or switch among them. Jasmine provides basic database facilities such as transaction management.

7.2.2 Implementation

The Jasmine system has a layered architecture consisting of *object management* and *data management* (See Figure 7.1). The object management layer allows modeling and manipulation of objects. In particular, this layer has *object buffers* which can efficiently manage objects in main memory. The data management layer allows transaction management and page buffer management as database functions.

The data management layer is a general-purpose database management system which extends relational databases [YAMA89]. This enables the user to define and access *nested relations* [ROTH88] as well as flat relations. This layer provides *nest* and *unnest* *operations* for relations in addition to reference and update. The system provides sequential, B-tree-based, and hash-based access to both flat and nested relations. A *clustered index* can be implemented by storing whole tuples into B-tree relations. A *nonclustered index* can be implemented by storing only keys and tuple identifiers into B-tree relations.

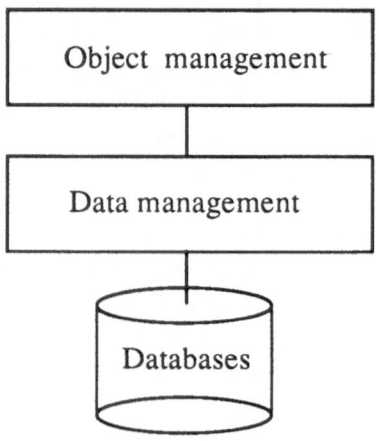

Figure 7.1. Jasmine architecture.

Objects are mapped into relations as follows. All intrinsic instances of a class are stored in a relation by corresponding attributes to fields. Intrinsic instances include inherited and non-inherited attributes. Multiple values are stored in multiple-valued fields, the simplest form of nested relations. Classes are stored in nested relations as they have nested structures.

The user can specify logical page sizes for each relation. Each class has its own page size. A class normally inherits the page size of its superclass. However, if necessary, the page size can be enlarged. There is no limitation to the number and length of tuples and fields although whole tuples must be contained in one page. This enables the user to optimally store and access large-scale media data such as images. Operations and tests on fields of relations are treated as user-defined functions in the data management layer and compiled into operations on data in page buffers.

Object queries are translated into relational operations such as selection and join. During this process, they are optimized. Object expressions generate several joins whose execution order is dynamically determined. Joins are usually processed based on hashing.

If an index is attached to fields, it is used for selection and join.

Page buffers are appropriate for access to homogeneous data, but inappropriate for access to related heterogeneous data such as complex objects. Therefore, the object management layer provides object buffers. Objects, when accessed for the first time, are fetched from databases in secondary memory to page buffers in the data management layer. Only the needed data comes to the object buffers from page buffers. Object identifiers are represented as a triplet of database number, class number, and instance number. The object identifiers of objects fetched into object buffers are translated into addresses in main memory. This eliminates the need for joins of relations and enables direct access of complex objects. Objects in object buffers also have tuple identifiers. If there are any updated objects in the object buffers, they are written back to the page buffers using the tuple identifiers at the end of the transaction.

Before a set-oriented query is evaluated, any updated objects associated with the query in object buffers are moved to the page buffers. Then the query is evaluated against the page buffers. Unlike Jasmine, Orion [KIM90] evaluates the same query both on object buffers and page buffers and integrates the results. Our approach needs only one evaluation scheme, so the system can be more compact.

A query on nonleaf classes in a class hierarchy is translated into multiple queries on relations. Simple methods specified in a query, such as manipulation of attributes, are transformed into operations on fields of relations. These can be executed more efficiently on page buffers because it reduces unnecessary data transfer between page and object buffers. On the other hand, more complex methods, such as manipulation of heterogeneous objects of complex objects, are more efficiently evaluated in object buffers. Methods appearing in the condition part are similarly processed. Jasmine efficiently executes methods by combining object and page buffers unlike other OODBs.

7.3 Issues for Engineering Tasks

Engineering tasks include planning, design, experiments, and manufacturing. However, only a fraction of these are supported by computers. Thus, conventional CAD systems handle only part of primary design data, focusing on drawing processes. Planning and conceptual design prior to drawing are not supported. Information relevant to the entire engineering task is not managed. In order to increase the total productivity and reliability of engineering tasks, we should support these processes and manage engineering information by computers. In the rest of this section, we analyze characteristics of engineering tasks, focusing on important requirements for their supports.

Design processes necessitate both structural and behavioral representation of primary design data. As structural aspects, we must represent relationships between design objects and their components and relationships between similar design objects. We call these *component* (or *aggregation*) *relationships* and *generalization relationships* [SMIT77]. Direct support of these relationships is a basic requirement for design data management. As behavioral aspects, we must describe *design constraints* which hold between design objects. We must also describe *design procedures* to generate candidate solutions which satisfy such design constraints. We call this advanced requirement *intelligent CAD support.*

Throughout the engineering processes, we must create, retrieve, and manipulate information, such as engineering documents, relevant to primary design data. Even designers must spend most of their time by doing such tasks. Engineering documents consist of large-scale data of various types such as numbers, character strings, graphics, and images. So a variety of data types must be integrated. Heterogeneous media data must be treated uniformly and flexibly. Relationships between heterogeneous media data must also be managed. As engineering documents will be subject to revision, we must maintain consistency constraints between related media data.

These requirements are summarized as follows.

(1) Design data management: We must manage large-scale primary design data, focusing on direct representation of component relationships and generalization relationships between them.

(2) Intelligent CAD support: We must describe design constraints and design procedures as design knowledge.

(3) Engineering information management: We must uniformly and flexibly manage heterogeneous media data. We must maintain consistency constraints between related media data during design revisions.

These requirements are not comprehensive (for example, support for cooperative work by a group of designers is also important), but vital for support of engineering tasks. In the rest of this chapter, we describe our OODB approaches to each of the above requirements.

7.4 Design Data Management

Design data management includes direct representation of component relationships between design objects and generalization relationships between similar design objects. These facilities can be implemented by complex object modeling and class hierarchies of OODB. For example, we model design objects using Jasmine as follows. The attribute Part of the class UNIT denotes that units consist of multiple components (See

Figure 7.2). The attribute Super of the class PISTON, which supports generalization, denotes that pistons inherit attributes of components. OODBs can reduce redundancy of schemas and represent component relationships directly in this way.

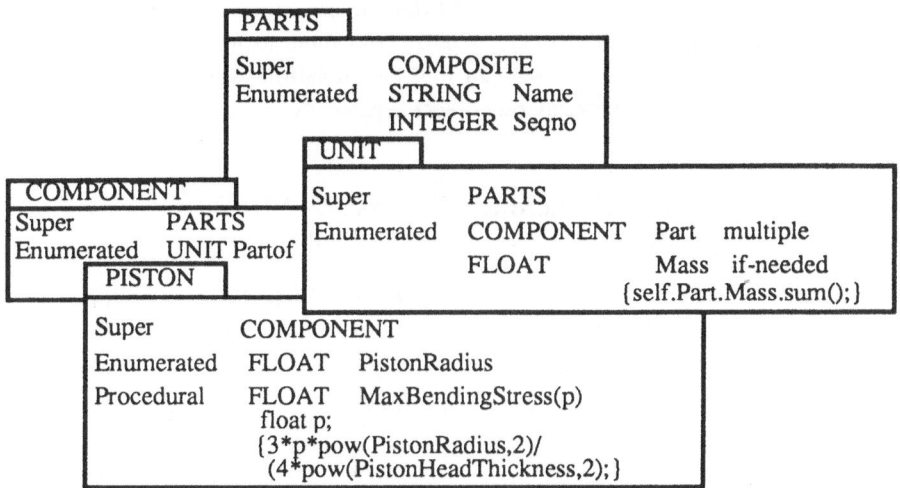

Figure 7.2. Class definitions.

Note that the semantics which the user gives to component relationships vary from application to application while those of generalization relationships are the same. Therefore, Jasmine has no built-in semantics of component relationships. Part is just a user-defined attribute for Jasmine. Instead, the user can provide application-specific semantics to properties and methods as demons in Jasmine. For example, there is a consistency constraint such that components can only exist when associated units exist (this constraint doesn't necessarily hold in bottom-up design where components are prior to units). This constraint can be implemented by specifying programs instantiating components as an after demon of the instantiate method of the class UNIT and programs destroying components as a before demon of the destroy method of UNIT. As another example, such a constraint that the mass of a unit is the sum of the mass of its components can be implemented as if-needed demon attached to the attribute Mass of UNIT (See Figure 7.2). This can maintain the mass of units in a consistent state. Jasmine demons manage user-specified application-specific consistency constraints. This facility is more difficult to provide in relational databases and other OODBs.

The user can usually describe engineering tasks completely by using OODBs. First, OODBs can represent dynamic characteristics of design data as methods. For example, the method MaxBendingStress calculates the maximum bending stress imposed on a piston head (See Figure 7.2). OODBs can not only define such application-specific functions but can provide generic operations such as retrieval and update by encapsulating them as system-defined methods of general objects. Flexible retrieval of design data is important in engineering applications. Jasmine allows the user to retrieve data from complex, large-scale data sets by providing a set-oriented query language (See Figure 7.3). Jasmine also facilitates advanced flexible searching by allowing the user to specify methods in queries. Generally, OODBs contribute to increase productivity in application development as the user can make application programs by combining methods and queries without considering object persistency.

UNIT where UNIT .Mass < 11.0
and UNIT.Part.Name = "conrod"

(retrieve units which are under 11 units
of mass and have a part named "conrod")

Figure 7.3. A query.

7.5 Intelligent   CAD Support

Although there are rather sophisticated CAD systems supporting drawing in design, they do not sufficiently improve the total productivity of design processes. The designer should be able to represent a collection of design constraints and various design methods for generating candidate solutions to design constraints. As constraints are rarely satisfied at the beginning, the designer should be able to specify what to do when the constraints are unsatisfactory. This ability is called intelligent CAD support. Here we describe an approach using Jasmine for intelligent CAD support.

We provide objects, called *design goals*, for management of design constraints in addition to design objects. The user can describe design constraints, design methods, and advice for constraint failures in design goal objects. The user can specify a collection of constraints on attributes of design objects as design constraints. The user can choose among database (table) retrieval, calculation based on other attributes, generation, and user input as design methods. The user can invoke other design goals or its own. These descriptions constitute a part of design knowledge.

The system finds solutions which satisfy the constraints, based on a network consisting of design goals and dependency relationships between them. Such a dependency network is created prior to finding the solutions. During that time, error checks are done. Figure 7.4 (a) depicts a part of a dependency network. Figure 7.4 (b) describes a part of design goal definition for determining the value of the attribute

PistonHeadThickness of PISTON. The constraints in the design goal describe what this attribute must satisfy. The design method generates candidate values from the initial value and increase value. The advice for failure of the third constraint sends its own goal a message to increase in value or sends a message to decrease in value to the goal for Diameter of PISTON.

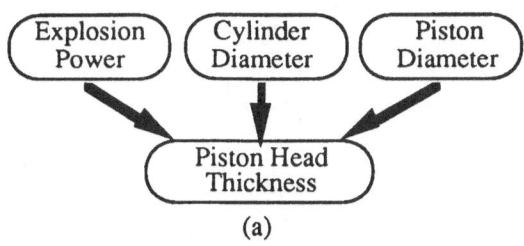

(a)

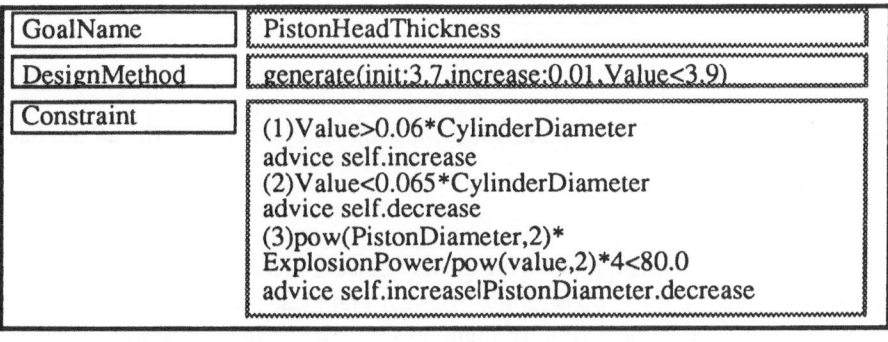

GoalName	PistonHeadThickness
DesignMethod	generate(init:3.7,increase:0.01,Value<3.9)
Constraint	(1)Value>0.06*CylinderDiameter advice self.increase (2)Value<0.065*CylinderDiameter advice self.decrease (3)pow(PistonDiameter,2)* ExplosionPower/pow(value,2)*4<80.0 advice self.increase|PistonDiameter.decrease

(b)

Figure 7.4. Design goal. (a) a dependency network. (b) goal definition.

Our approach to constraint failure is called *knowledge-based backtrack* in that the user controls the backtracking directly. In contrast, in most *constraint programming languages* [LELE88] the user only describes constraints and leaves constraint satisfaction to the system. That is, the satisfaction mechanism is hidden from to the user. Such a black box scheme is inappropriate for design because techniques of constraint satisfaction are a part of design knowledge. So we provide a scheme such as design goals where the user can describe design knowledge directly and the system can interpret the knowledge. Although pure OODBs provides no direct support for constraint management, we can implement constraint management just by adding objects for constraint management.

ConrodGeo.y= CrankGeo.CrankHead1.center.y
ConrodGeo.z=CrankGeo.CrankHead1.center.z+
  CrankGeo.CrankArmThickness+
  (CrankGeo.CrankPinLength-ConrodGeo.ConrodThickness)/2

(a)

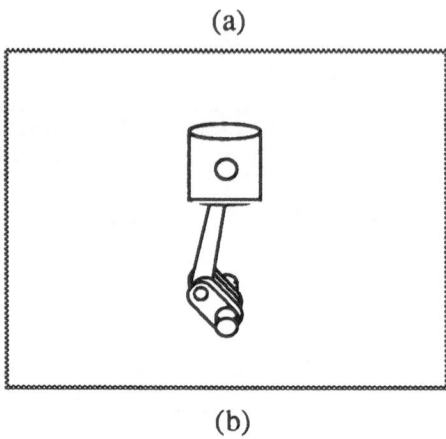

(b)

Figure 7.5. Constraint-based animation. (a) a geometric constraint. (b) an animation still.

Plans or graphics associated with design objects are created, based on design solutions inferred from the constraints. As with graphics, there are also geometrical constraints such as the connection of components. We can make graphics of possible states by resolving such geometrical constraints. By repeating this process for each graphic at different times, we can make an animation series to facilitate primitive simulation in conceptual design. We call this approach *constraint-based animation*. For example, Figure 7.5 (a) depicts a part of the geometrical constraints and Figure 7.5 (b) depicts an animation still resolving such constraints. Note that graphics data must be updated if associated design objects are updated. This can be implemented by supplying if-updated demons to attributes of design objects.

7.6 Engineering Information Management

Creation, retrieval, and manipulation of engineering information is the largest part of engineering. Management of such engineering documents improves the total productivity and reliability of engineering tasks. Engineering documents consist of various data, such as texts, figures, tables, and relationships between them, so a hypermedia approach seems promising for engineering document management.

Hypermedia systems, such as NoteCards [HALA88], have simple data models consisting of nodes and links that allow data retrieval by link traversal. However, most current hypermedia systems, if they were applied to complex, large-scale applications such as engineering tasks, have problems with complex object modeling, efficient management of large-scale media data, flexible searching facilities, programming facilities, and change management related to application evolution. Here we describe an OODB approach to the basic functions and advanced issues of hypermedia in general.

Media data can be added to OODBs easily. Basic media such as graphics, images, and text are defined as objects. Long data is stored in attributes of byte strings. In Jasmine, the user can optimally adjust the maximum length of data contained within one page by specifying the page size of each object. Operations on media are defined as object methods. Heterogeneous media data can be operated on uniformly using polymorphism.

Presentation of media objects and their structures and contents are different although they are related. That is, the mapping between them is non-trivial. For example, presentation of complex objects needs simultaneous presentation of various types of attribute values. To this, we must define composite media data as complex objects. The user must be able to directly access data by pointing with the mouse. This function, called *direct manipulation* of media data, corresponds to link traversal. To allow direct manipulation, we must manage physical structures for composite media, consisting of geometrical information such as display areas, in addition to their logical structures. We represent pairs of OIDs and display areas as area objects. If the user selects displayed media data, the system selects an object whose display area contains the point by invoking the search method of associated area objects. The user can manipulate the selected data by sending dedicated messages.

The user sometimes needs to access objects contained in text objects such as design goals associated with design guidebooks (See Figure 7.6). Conventionally, this is implemented by managing their OIDs and display areas as described above. In contrast, we have taken an approach where we create a table consisting of keywords appearing within texts and OIDs of associated objects in addition to texts. If the user drags a keyword string in a presented text, the system selects the OID of the associated object by searching the table. This approach eliminates the need for recalculating display areas associated with updated texts and for managing multiple entries for objects recurring in texts.

Our work using Jasmine is an OODB approach to current hypermedia issues [ISHI90]. Direct manipulation of hypermedia is not enough for complex, large-scale engineering tasks although it is extremely useful. The user should be able to do flexible searching using complex conditions and procedures. In Jasmine the user can do advanced searching such as structural and content searches by invoking dedicated methods in queries. To manage change associated with application evolution, we allow the user to specify queries within methods in order to define virtual nodes and links. For example, Figure 7.7 (a) defines a virtual link. Figure 7.7 (b) depicts use of the virtual link through an end-user interface. The query is also represented as an object. Ad hoc queries can be interactively interpreted while routine queries can be compiled and efficiently executed. For complex object modeling, the user can maintain consistency constraints between heterogeneous media objects by using demons. For example, if the value of an attribute of a design object, such as PistonHeadThickness, is updated, the associated graphic objects, such as plans, are updated by an if-updated demon attached to the attribute.

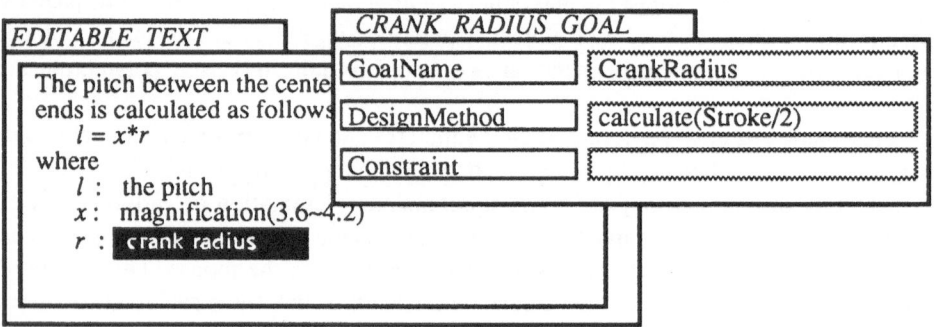

Figure 7.6. Traversal of objects contained within text.

Providing a general-purpose user interface is mandatory for application development using OODBs. The user should be able to customize a general user interface for his own needs. We provide a library consisting of system-defined media and window objects which the user can customize through inheritance and addition of attributes to build personalized user interface. O2 [DEUX90] provides a library for customizing user interfaces of OODB applications, but unlike our approach, the library is not implemented as objects.

7.7 Conclusion

7.7.1 Related work

HyperCAD is a prototype intelligent CAD system, which embodies Jasmine approaches to engineering tasks as described above. KRISYS [DEBL89] is similar to HyperCAD/Jasmine in that KRISYS provides a knowledge base management system based on the integration of database and artificial intelligence technology for the construction of advanced CAD systems. Like HyperCAD, KRISYS provides facilities for abstraction mechanisms such as generalization, classification, aggregation, and methods for behavioral modeling, and demons for integrity constraints. KRISYS, however, lacks a facility for managing constraints such as design and geometric constraints.

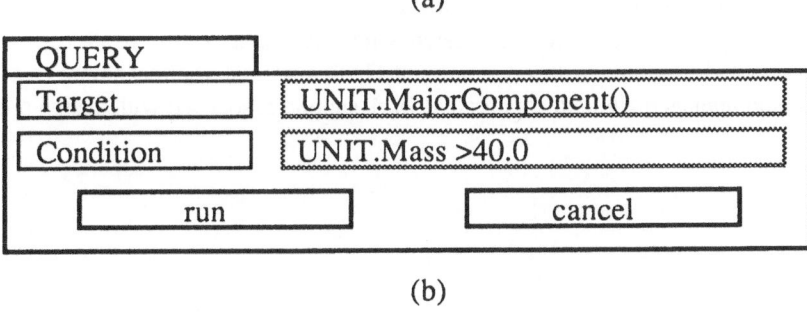

UNIT
  Procedural COMPONENT MajorComponent ( ) multiple
  {self.Part where self.Part.Mass.sum() > self.Mass*0.1
       groupby self.Part.Mass;}

(define major components of a unit as components whose group total mass makes up more than 10 % of the mass of the unit)

(a)

QUERY	
Target	UNIT.MajorComponent()
Condition	UNIT.Mass >40.0
run	cancel

(b)

Figure 7.7. Virtual link. (a) definition. (b) usage.

HyperCAD is similar to constraint-based design systems such as VT/SALT [MARC88], AIR-CYL/DSPL [BROW89], and PRIDE [MITT86a] [MITT86b]. Like HyperCAD, SALT and DSPL are generic systems which enable the user to define specific CAD systems such as VT for elavator design and AIR-CYL for air cylinder design. PRIDE is an expert system for the design of paper transports inside copiers. All these systems use a knowledge-based approach to design revisions when constraint satisfaction fails. VT/SALT allows the user to provide preference for fixes; the system determines the order of backtracking according to the preference rating provided by the user. AIR-CYL/DSPL enables the user to describe failure handlers within constraints. When there are several alternatives, the system takes a least backup strategy and moves back to the most recently established decision point. PRIDE also allows the user to define advice for revision in addition to system-generated advice. PRIDE enables the user to explore different alternatives simultaneously by maintaining multiple design contexts while HyperCAD, VT/SALT, and AIR-CYL/DSPL provide design alternatives sequentially. VT/SALT, AIR-CYL/DSPL, and PRIDE are largely different from HyperCAD in that these three systems lack facilities for abstraction mechanisms, behavioral modeling, and geometric constraint management.

7.7.2 Summary

We described the functionality and implementation of our prototype OODB, Jasmine. Then we discussed the requirements for supporting engineering tasks and described our OODB approach to them, focusing on management of constraints such as description, satisfaction, and maintenance. We call this the *constraint object-oriented approach*. This has been realized in a prototype intelligent CAD system, called *HyperCAD*, which consists of more than one hundred classes defined by Jasmine. OODBs, however, have just been developed, so there are very few reports of real applications [KETA90] [KUWA91]. We would like to continue our work, not only to verify the validity of OODB approaches to engineering applications but to also give feedback to OODBs from the experiences. Some issues associated with CAD that were not addressed in this chapter include linkage with conventional CAD systems, version management, long transaction management, and cooperative work support associated with design processes.

Chapter 8
CONCLUSION

8.1 Related Work

Jasmine has resulted from work in different fields - data modeling work in the database field, object work in the programming language field, and frame work in the AI field. In particular, Jasmine shares a lot of functionality with advanced database systems: functional data model-based DBMSs such as DAPLEX [SHIP81], IRIS [FISH87] [LYNG87], object-oriented DBMSs such as GemStone [MAIE86], ORION [BANE87] [KIM88] [KIM89], Encore [SHAW89], O2 [CLUE89], semantic data model-based DBMSs such as TAXIS [MYLO80] [NIXO87], SIM [JAGA88], and extensible DBMSs such as POSTGRES [STON86] [STON87].

First we compare Jasmine with other work from the viewpoint of data modeling. Jasmine borrows a function concept from DAPLEX. The set of DAPLEX, however, allows no duplicates of elements unlike Jasmine. IRIS is similar to Jasmine in that IRIS constrains multiple superclasses to overlapping classes and considers a type and a function as an instance of system-supplied types. However, IRIS supports no active databases. Integration of functions and frames makes the Jasmine model more expressive than those of the other two. The fact that Jasmine methods can be programmed in a unified, general-purpose programming language makes Jasmine the most powerful of the group.

Jasmine is similar to GemStone, ORION, and O2 in that they use object-oriented data models. GemStone distinguishes between sets and classes unlike Jasmine. ORION focuses on representation of complex objects. O2 principally distinguishes between values and objects and extends the notion of values to complex objects represented by nested relations like Jasmine. TAXIS and SIM aim to efficiently implement a semantic data model by restricting and clarifying its semantics like Jasmine. However, TAXIS incorporates a metaclass to represent intentional knowledge while Jasmine adheres to a class. SIM lacks representation of behavioral knowledge. POSTGRES attempts to incorporate behavioral knowledge, but POSTGRES adheres to a relational model. None of the above models can represent incomplete knowledge in our context.

Next we compare from the viewpoint of the language. IRIS, GemStone, ORION, and O2 provide SQL-like query languages. Unlike Jasmine, IRIS emphasizes more on compatibility with a relational query language. GemStone attempts to provide a programming environment to develop applications like Jasmine. However, GemStone requires a collection class to associatively retrieve objects. Unlike Jasmine, ORION limits a query result to a subset of a single class and provides no way to construct tuples consisting of several classes. O2 defines the semantics of the language by use of algebraic operators like Jasmine. However, O2 adopts the functional composition notation instead of the dot notation. Encore proposes object algebraic operators like Jasmine but Encore emphasizes more on query optimization based on its algebra while Jasmine aims to define the semantics of the query language based on its algebra. SIM doesn't allow the user to define new operators. TAXIS can define a transaction in a general-purpose programming language and can operate on intentional knowledge like Jasmine. POSTGRES allows the dot notation and allows the user to define new functions like Jasmine, but POSTGRES distinguishes between system-defined commands and user-supplied functions.

From the implementation point of view, we compare Jasmine. IRIS has a layered architecture like Jasmine. However, IRIS uses a traditional database system which cannot support nested relations. GemStone is a collection of dedicated subsystems.

ORION provides object buffers in addition to page buffers like Jasmine. However, ORION evaluates the same query separately on the object buffers and page buffers and then integrates the results. SIM is layered but is based on network databases. TAXIS takes the maximum advantage of the compiling technique like Jasmine.

We summarize the features of current commercial object-oriented database systems and industrial research prototypes as follows.

Ontos [ONTO89] provides a persistent object store for C++ programs. An object first accessed by an application program is automatically activated; the object is translated into in-memory representation and object identifiers are changed into C++ pointers in place. Ontos supports an extension of SQL for queries.

ObjectStore [OBJE90] also makes C++ objects databases. Any data in C++ programs can be persistent. A query, as an extension to C++, consists of a collection of objects and C++ Boolean expressions.

GemStone [BRET89] starts from the attempt to make Smalltalk-80 programs databases. The GemStone data model is based on Smalltalk-80 and supports only single inheritance. In addition to C, C++, Smalltalk-80 interfaces, GemStone provides a programming interface called OPAL. GemStone distinguishes between a class and a collection of objects. A query expressed by OPAL is formulated against a collection of objects. GemStone provides transactions, concurrency control, recovery, and schema modification. Object joins are processed by B-tree indexes. The process called Gem provides an object model and a program complier. The Stone process provides disk I/O, transactions, and concurrency control.

ORION [KIM90] provides multiple inheritance, composite objects, versions, queries, and schema evolution. ORION is built in Lisp on a secondary storage system which provides facilities for segment and page management. ORION provides a programming interface to an object-oriented extension of Lisp. A query returns a collection of instances of a single class. Mapping object identifiers to pointers is done by extensible hashing. A query with attributes of nonleaf classes is processed by use of a class-hierarchy index. ORION evaluates a query against the object and page buffers and merges the results into one. ORION emphasizes on the semantics of versioning, schema modification, and composite objects.

O2 [DEUX90] supports multiple inheritance and a query language. An O2 object contains a value, a list, a set, and a tuple as an attribute value. O2 is used through an object-oriented extension of C called CO2. The query language is defined rather formally. The query retrieves and composes a list, a set, and a tuple. O2 is implemented on top of WiSS (Wisconsin Storage System) in C. WiSS provides persistency, disk management, and concurrency control for flat records. O2 uses physical identifiers of WiSS records as object identifiers. Like ORION, O2 adopts a dual buffer management scheme. O2 uses a hash table to manage in-memory objects and a class-hierarchy index to process queries against nonleaf classes.

IRIS [LYNG87] is based on the DAPLEX functional model. Properties or methods defined by a class are represented as functions on the class. Functions are stored or derived from other functions. IRIS supports multiple inheritance, versions, schema evolution, and queries. Query optimization is done by rule bases. IRIS is implemented on a relational storage system called HP-SQL in C. IRIS has C and Lisp interfaces, but supports no integration with object-oriented programming languages. IRIS provides an object-oriented extension to SQL for queries. An IRIS object can have multiple types (classes) unlike other systems.

8.2 Summary

In this thesis we described an object-oriented DBMS called Jasmine, focusing on the object model, object manipulation language, and implementation. Then we discussed object-oriented database approaches to advanced applications such as artificial intelligence, hypermedia, and engineering. We would like to apply our object-oriented

DBMS Jasmine to various real-world problems, not only to verify the validity of object-oriented database approaches but to also give feedback to Jasmine from the experiences.

Our future plans include research on technical issues associated with explorative aspects of advanced applications such as design: The performance improvement of complex object access, and the incorporation of version management, constraint management, long transaction management, and view management in a distributed environment.

Exploration in CAD applications based on simulation and versioning requires intensive access of design data represented as complex objects. Therefore, clustering, buffering, and query optimization issues relevant to complex objects must be solved to improve the performance of complex object access. Version management is mandatory for explorative applications, but concepts of versions differ from application to application. It is important to propose generic concepts of versions from which specific versions can be derived. Description and satisfaction of constraints such as design and geometric constraints helps the user explore design alternatives and generate an animation series. It is necessary to incorporate generalized constraint management [ISHI93b]. Conventional transactions are unacceptable for exploration. We must provide support for long transactions in addition to conventional transactions. Moreover, to support exploration in a cooperative environment, we must provide a basic distribution facility and view support which allows the user to look at schemas defined by other users differently from the original ones [ISHI92].

Appendix
QUERY EXPRESSION SYNTAX

(1) query-expression ::= target-clause [where-clause] [groupby-clause]

(2) target-clause ::= object-expression
       | " [" object-expression "," object-expression-list "]"

(3) where-clause ::= "where" condition

(4) groupby-clause ::= "groupby" object-expression-list

(5) object-expression ::= class-name | class-name "." attribute-names

(6) attribute-names ::= attribute-name | attribute-name "." attribute-names
       | "{" attribute-names "}"

(7) attribute-name ::= property-name
       | method-name "(" [parameter-list] ")"

(8) parameter-list ::= parameter | parameter "," parameter-list

(9) object-expression-list ::= object-expression
       | object-expression "," object-expression-list

(10) condition ::= boolean-term | boolean-term "or" condition

(11) boolean-term ::= boolean-factor | boolean-factor "and" boolean-term

(12) boolean-factor ::= boolean-primary

(13) boolean-primary ::= predicate | "(" condition ")"

(14) predicate ::= comparison-expression ["All"] comparator
                         comparison-expression

(15) comparison-expression ::= object-expression | literal

(16) comparator ::= "=" | "<=" | ">=" | "<" | ">" | "!="

Bibliography

[ABIT87] ABITEBOUL, S., AND HULL, R. IFO: A formal semantic model. *ACM Trans. Database Syst. 12*, 4 (Dec. 1987). ACM, New York, 1987, 525-565.

[AGRA89] AGRAWAL, R., AND GEHANI, N.H. ODE (Object Database and Environment): The Language and the Data Model. In *Proceedings of the 1989 ACM SIGMOD Conference* (Portland, OR., June 1989). ACM, New York, 1989, 36-45.

[BALL84] BALLARD, B.W., ET AL. LDC-1: A Transportable, Knowledge-Based Natural Language Processor for Office Environments. *ACM Trans. Office Information Systems, 2*, 1, (1984). ACM, New York, 1984, 1-25.

[BANC86] BANCILHON, F., AND KHOSHAFIAN, S. A calculus for complex objects. In *Proceedings of the 1986 ACM PODS Conference* (Cambridge, MA., Mar. 1986). ACM, New York, 1986, 53-59.

[BANE87] BANERJEE, J., ET AL. Data model issues for object-oriented applications. *ACM Trans. Office Inf. Syst. 5*, 1 (Jan. 1987). ACM, New York, 1987, 3-26.

[BARR81] BARR, A., AND FEIGENBAUM, F.A. *The Handbook of Artificial Intelligence* vol.1, William Kaufmann Inc., 1981.

[BATE84] BATES, M. Accessing a Database with a Transportable Natural Language Interface. In *Proceedings of the IEEE 1st Conference on Artificial Intelligence Applications* (1984). IEEE, Los Alamitos, CA., 1984, 9-12.

[BATO88] BATORY, D. S., LEUNG, T. Y., AND WISE, T. E. Implementation concept for an extensible data model and data language. *ACM Trans. Database Syst. 13*, 3 (Sept. 1988). ACM, New York, 1988, 231-262.

[BLOO87] BLOOM, T., AND ZDONIK, S.B. Issues in the design of object-oriented database programming languages. In *Proceedings of the 2nd OOPSLA Conference* (Orlando, FL., 1987). ACM, New York, 1987, 441-451.

[BOBR81] BOBROW, D.G., AND STEFIK M. The LOOPS Manual, Xerox PARC, Knowledge-based VLSI Design Group Memo, 1981.

[BRET89] BRETL, R., ET AL. The GemStone Data Management System. In *Object-Oriented Concepts, Applications, and Databases*, W. KIM, AND F. LOCHOVSKY Eds., Addison-Wesley, 1989.

[BROW89] BROWN, D.C., AND CHANDRASEKARAN, B. *Design problem solving: knowledge structures and control strategies.* Morgan Kaufmann Publishers, Inc., San Mateo, CA., 1989.

[BURG80] BURGER, J.F. Semantic Database Mapping in EUFID. In *Proceedings of the 1980 ACM SIGMOD Conference* (1980). ACM, New York, 1980, 67-74.

[CARA89] CARANDO, P. Shadow: Fusing Hypertext with AI. *IEEE Expert*, *4*, 4 (Winter 1989). IEEE, Los Alamitos, CA., 1989, 65-78.

[CARE88] CAREY, M. J., DEWITT, D.J., AND VANDENBERG, S. L. A data model and query language for EXODUS. In *Proceedings of the 1988 ACM SIGMOD Conference* (Chicago, IL., June 1988). ACM, New York, 1988, 413-423.

[CLUE89] CLUET, S. ET AL. Reloop, an algebra-based query language for object-oriented database system. In *Proceedings of the 1989 DOOD Conference* (Kyoto, Japan, Dec. 1989), 294-313.

[DATE81] DATE, C.J. Referential integrity. In *Proceedings of the 7th VLDB Conference* (Cannes, France, Sept. 1981). IEEE, Los Alamitos, CA., 1981, 2-12.

[DATE90] DATE, C.J. *An Introduction to Database Systems*, *Volume 1*, Addison-Wesley, Reading, Mass., 1990.

[DEBL89] DEBLOCH, S. ET AL. KRISYS: KBMS Support for Better CAD Systems. In *Proceedings of the 2nd International Conference on Data and Knowledge systems for Manufacturing and Engineering* (Gaithersburg, MD., October 1989). IEEE, Los Alamitos, CA., 1989, 172-182.

[DELI86] DELISLE, N. AND SCHWARTZ, M.   Neptune: A Hypertext system for CAD applications. in *Proceedings of the 1986 ACM SIGMOD Conference* (Washington, D.C., May 1986). ACM, New York, 1986, 132-142.

[DELI87] DELISLE, N. AND SCHWARTZ, M.   Contexts: A Partitioning Concept for Hypertext. *ACM Trans. Office Information System, 5,* 2(April 1987). ACM, New York, 1987, 168-186.

[DEUX90] DEUX, O., ET AL.   The Story of O2. *IEEE Transactions on Knowledge and Data Engineering. 2*, 1 (March 1990). IEEE, Los Alamitos, CA., 1990, 91-108.

[FISH87] FISHMAN, D. H., ET AL.   IRIS: An object-oriented database management system. *ACM Trans. Office Inf. Syst. 5*, 1 (Jan. 1987). ACM, New York, 1987, 48-69.

[GOLD83] GOLDBERG, A. AND ROBSON, D.   *Smalltalk-80: The language and its implementation.* Addison-Wesley, Reading, MA., 1983.

[GOOD87] GOODMAN, D. *The Complete HyperCard Handbook.* Bantam Books, New York, 1987.

[GUTT84] GUTTMAN, A.   R-trees: A dynamic index structure for spatial searching. In *Proceedings of the 1984 ACM SIGMOD Conference* (Boston, MA., June 1984). ACM, New York, 1984, 47-57.

[HALA88] HALASZ, F. G.   Reflections on notecards: Seven issues for the next generation of hypermedia systems. *Comm. ACM 31*, 7 (July 1988). ACM, New York, 1988, 836-852.

[HAMM81] HAMMER, M., AND MCLEOD, D.   Database description with SDM: A semantic database model. *ACM Trans. Database Syst. 6*, 3 (Sept. 1981). ACM, New York, 1981, 351-386.

[HASK82] HASKIN, R. L., AND LORIE, R. A.   On extending the functions of a relational database system. In *Proceedings of the 1982 ACM SIGMOD Conference* (Orlando, FL., June 1982). ACM, New York, 1982, 207-212.

[HAYE84] HAYES, D.J.   Entity-Oriented Parsing. In *Proceedings of the 10th International Conference on Computational Linguistics.* 1984, 212-217.

[HEND78] HENDRIX, G.G., ET AL. Developing a natural language interface to complex data. *ACM Trans. Database Syst. 3*, 2(1978). ACM, New York, 1978, 105-147.

[HEND81] HENDLER, J., ET AL. Issues in the development of natural language front-ends. In *Proceedings of the AFIPS 1981 NCC, 50*, 1981, 643-648.

[ISHI86] ISHIKAWA, H., IZUMIDA, Y., YOSHINO, T., HOSHIAI, T., AND MAKINOUCHI, A. A Knowledge-based approach to design a portable natural language interface to database systems. In *Proceedings of the IEEE Data Engineering Conference* (1986). IEEE, Los Alamitos, CA., 1986, 134-143.

[ISHI87] ISHIKAWA, H., IZUMIDA, Y., YOSHINO, T., HOSHIAI, T., AND MAKINOUCHI, A. KID: Designing a knowledge-based natural language interface. *IEEE Expert, 2*, 2 (summer 1987). IEEE, Los Alamitos, CA., 1987, 57-71.

[ISHI88] ISHIKAWA, H., SUZUKI, F., AND MAKINOUCHI, A. Object-oriented multimedia knowledge base management system: Design and implementation. *Proceedings of the 2nd International Symposium on Interoperable Information Systems* (Tokyo, Japan, Nov. 1988). INTAP, Japan, 1988, 195-202.

[ISHI90] ISHIKAWA, H. An object-oriented knowledge base approach to a next generation of hypermedia system. In *Proceedings of the 35th IEEE COMPCON Conference* (San Francisco, CA., 1990). IEEE, Los Alamitos, CA., 1990, 520-527.

[ISHI91a] ISHIKAWA, H., IZUMIDA, Y., AND KAWATO, N. An Object-Oriented Database: System and Applications. In *Proceedings of the IEEE Pacific Rim Conference on Communications, Computers, and Signal Processing* (Victoria, B.C., CANADA). IEEE, Los Alamitos, CA., 1991, 288-291.

[ISHI91b] ISHIKAWA, H., IZUMIDA, Y., AND KAWATO, N. Object-oriented database approaches to engineering tasks (in Japanese). *Journal Information Processing Society of Japan, 32*, 5(1991). IPS Japan, 1991, 593-601.

[ISHI92] ISHIKAWA, H., IZUMIDA, Y., KAWATO, N., AND HAYASHI, T. An Object-Oriented Database System and its View Mechanism for Schema Integration, In *Proceedings of the 2nd Far-East Workshop on Future Database Systems* (Kyoto, Japan, April 1992). World Scientific, Singapore, 1992, 194-200.

[ISHI93a] ISHIKAWA, H., SUZUKI, F., KOZAKURA, F., MAKINOUCHI, A., MIYAGISHIMA, M., IZUMIDA, Y., AOSHIMA, M, AND YAMANE, Y. The Model, Language, and Implementation of an Object-Oriented Multimedia Knowledge Base Management System. *ACM Trans. Database Syst. 18*, 1 (March 1993). ACM, New York, 1993, 1-50.

[ISHI93b] ISHIKAWA, H., AND KUBOTA, K. An Active Object-Oriented Database: A Multi-Paradigm Approach to Constraint Management. In *Proceedings of the 19th VLDB Conference* (Dublin, Ireland, 1993). VLDB endowment, 1993.

[JAGA88] JAGANNATHAN, D., ET AL. SIM: A database system based on the semantic data model. In *Proceedings of the 1988 ACM SIGMOD Conference* (Chicago, IL., June 1988). ACM, New York, 1988, 46-55.

[JAKO86] JAKOBSON, G., ET AL. An Intelligent Database Assistant. *IEEE Expert, 1*, 2 (Summer 1986). IEEE, Los Alamitos, CA., 1986, 65-79.

[KAPL84] KAPLAN, S.J. Designing a Portable Natural Language Database Query System. *ACM Trans. Database Syst. 9*, 1 (March 1984). ACM, New York, 1984, 1-19.

[KETA90] KETABCHI, M.A., ET AL. Comparative Analysis of RDBMS and OODBMS: a Case Study. In *Proceedings of the 35th IEEE COMPCON Conference* (San Francisco, CA, 1990). IEEE, Los Alamitos, CA., 1990, 528-537.

[KHOS] KHOSHAFIAN, S., AND COPELAND, G. Object identity. In *Proceedings of the 1st OOPSLA Conference* (Portland, OR., 1986). ACM, New York, 1986, 406-416.

[KIM87] KIM, W., CHOU, H.-T., AND BANERJEE, J. Operations and implementation of complex objects. In *Proceedings of the IEEE Data Engineering Conference* (1987). IEEE, Los Alamitos, CA., 1987, 626-633.

[KIM88] KIM, W., ET AL. Integrating an object-oriented programming system with a database system. In *Proceedings of the 1988 OOPSLA Conference* (1988). ACM, New York, 1988, 142-152.

[KIM89] KIM, W. A model of queries for object-oriented databases. In *Proceedings of the 15th VLDB Conference* (Amsterdam, Holland, 1989). VLDB endowment, 1989, 423-432.

[KIM90] KIM, W., ET AL. Architecture of the ORION Next-generation Database System. *IEEE Transactions on Knowledge and Data Engineering. 2*, 1 (March 1990). IEEE, Los Alamitos, CA., 1990, 109-124.

[KITA89] KITAGAWA, H. AND KUNII, T. L. *The Unnormalized Relational Data Model for Office Form Processor Design.* Springer-Verlag, Tokyo, 1989.

[KUWA91] KUWANO, N., ET AL. Applications of Object-oriented Databases to Publishing Systems. In *Proceedings of the 2nd International Symposium on Database Systems for Advanced Applications.* (Tokyo, Japan, April 1991).

[LARS80] LARSON, P. -A. Linear hashing with partial expansions. In *Proceedings of the 6th VLDB Conference* (Montreal, Canada, 1980). ACM, New York, 1980, 224-232.

[LECL89] LECLUSE, C., AND RICHARD, P. The O2 database programming language. In *Proceedings of the 15th VLDB Conference* (Amsterdam, The Netherlands, Aug. 1989). VLDB Endowment, USA, 1989, 411-422.

[LELE88] LELER, W. *Constraint programming languages.* Addison-Wesley, Reading, MA., 1988.

[LYNG87] LYNGBAEK, P., AND VIANU, V. Mapping a semantic database model to the relational model. In *Proceedings of the 1987 ACM SIGMOD Conference* (San Francisco, CA., 1987). ACM, New York, 1987, 132-142.

[MAIE86] MAIER, D., ET AL. Development of an object-oriented DBMS. In *Proceedings of the 1st OOPSLA Conference* (Portland, OR., 1986). ACM, New York, 1986, 472-482.

[MAKI83] MAKINOUCHI, A., ET AL. Relational Database Management System RDB/V1 (in Japanese). *Trans. Information Processing Society of Japan, 24,* 1, 1983, 47-55.

[MARC88] MARCUS, S., STOUT, J., AND MCDERMOTT, J. VT: An Expert Elevator Designer That Uses Knowledge-Based Backtracking. *AI Magazine 9,* 1 (spring 1988), 95-114.

[MART83] MARTIN, P., APPELT, t D., AND PEREIRA, F. Transportability and Generality in a Natural Language Interface System. In *Proceedings of the IJCAI-83.* 1983, 573-581.

[MINS75] MINSKY, M. A. A framework for representing knowledge. In *The psychology of computer vision*. WINSTON, P. Ed., New York, McGraw-Hill, 1975.

[MITT86a] MITTAL, S., ET AL. PRIDE: An expert system for the design of paper handling systems. *IEEE Computer 19*, 7 (July 1986). IEEE, Los Alamitos, CA., 1986, 102-114.

[MITT86b] MITTAL, S., AND ARAYA, A. A Knowledge-Based Framework for Design. In *Proceedings of the AAAI-86 Conference* (Philadelphia, PA, Aug. 1986), 856-865.

[MORG83] MORGENSTERN, M. Active databases as a paradigm for enhanced computing environments. In *Proceedings of the 9th VLDB Conference* (Florence, Italy, Oct. 1983). VLDB endowment, 1983, 34-42.

[MYLO80] MYLOPOULOS, J., BERNSTEIN, P. A., AND WONG, H. K. T. A language facility for designing database intensive applications. *ACM Trans. Database Syst. 5*, 2 (June 1980). ACM, New York, 1980, 185-207.

[NIXO87] NIXON, B., ET AL. Implementation of a compiler for a semantic data model: Experiences with TAXIS. In *Proceedings of the 1987 ACM SIGMOD Conference* (San Francisco, CA., 1987). ACM, New York, 1987, 118-131.

[OBJE90] OBJECT DESIGN, INC. *An Introduction to ObjectStore*, Object Design, Inc., Burlington, Massachusetts, 1990.

[ONTO89] ONTOLOGIC, INC. *ONTOS Reference Manual,* Ontologic, Inc., Billerica, Massachusetts, 1989.

[ROTH87] ROTH, M. A., KORTH, H. F., AND BATORY, D. S. SQL/NF: A query language for ~1NF relational databases. *Inf. Syst. 12*, 1 (1987), 99-114.

[ROTH 88] ROTH, M. A., KORTH, H. F., AND SILBERSCHATZ, A. Extended algebra and calculus for nested relational databases *ACM Trans. Database Syst. 13*, 4 (Dec. 1988). ACM, New York, 1988, 389-417.

[SALV84] SALVETER, S. Supporting Natural Language Database Update by Modeling Real World Actions. In *Proceedings of 1st International Workshop on Expert Database Systems*. 1984, 275-297.

[SCHR84] SCHREFL, M., TJOA, A. M., AND WAGNER, R. R. Comparison-criteria for semantic data models. In *Proceedings of the IEEE Data Engineering Conference* (1984). IEEE, Los Alamitos, CA., 1984, 120-125.

[SHAW89] SHAW, G. M., AND ZDONIK, S. B. Object-oriented queries: equivalence and optimization. In *Proceedings of the 1989 DOOD Conference* (Kyoto, Japan, Dec. 1989), 264-278.

[SHIP81] SHIPMAN, D. The functional data model and the data language DAPLEX. *ACM Trans. Database Syst. 6*, 1 (Mar. 1981). ACM, New York, 1981, 140-173.

[SHNE83] SHNEIDERMAN, B. Direct manipulation: A step beyond programming languages. *IEEE Computer, 16*, 8 (Aug. 1983). IEEE, Los Alamitos, CA., 1983, 57-69.

[SMIT77] SMITH, J., AND SMITH, D. Database abstraction: Aggregation and generalization. *ACM Trans. Database Syst. 2*, 2 (June 1977). ACM, New York, 1977, 105-133.

[SMIT87] SMITH, K. E., ET AL.   Intermedia: A Case Study of the Differences Between Relational and Object-Oriented Database Systems. In *Proceedings of the 2nd OOPSLA Conference* (October 1987). ACM, New York, 1987, 452-465.

[SOND84] SONDHEIMER. N.K.,WEISCHEDEL,R.M., AND BOBROW, R.J. Semantic Interpretation Using KL-ONE.   In *Proceedings of the 10th International Conference on Computational Linguistics.* 1984, 101-107.

[STEF86] STEFIK, M., AND BOBROW, D. G.   Object-oriented programming: Themes and variations. *AI MAGAZINE, 6*, 4 (winter 1986), 40-62.

[STON86] STONEBRAKER, M., AND ROWE, L. A. The design of POSTGRES. In *Proceedings of the 1986 ACM SIGMOD Conference* (Washington, D.C., 1986). ACM, New York, 1986, 340-355.

[STON87] STONEBRAKER, M., ET AL. Extending a database with procedures. *ACM Trans. Database Syst. 12*, 3 (Sept. 1987). ACM, New York, 1987, 350-376.

[STRO86] STROUSTRUP, B.   *The C++ programming language*. Addison-Wesley, Reading, MA., 1986.

[TSUR84] TSUR, S., AND ZANIOLO, C. An Implementation of GEM - supporting a semantic data model on a relational back-end. In *Proceedings of the 1984 ACM SIGMOD Conference* (1984). ACM, New York, 1984, 286-295.

[WALT78] WALTZ, D.L.   An English language question answering system for a large relational data base. *Comm. ACM, 21*, 7(1978). ACM, New York, 1978, 526-539.

[YAMA85] YAMANE, Y. A hash join technique for relational database systems. In *Proceedings of the Foundation of Data Organization Conference* (Kyoto, Japan, May 1985), 388-398.

[YAMA89] YAMANE, Y., ET AL.   Design and evaluation of a high-speed extended relational database engine, XRDB. In *Proceedings of International Symposium on Database Systems for Advanced Applications* (Seoul, Korea, April 1989), 52-60.

[YANK88] YANKELOVICH, N., ET AL.   Intermedia: The concept and the Construction of a Seamless Information Environment. *IEEE Computer, 21,* 1(January 1988). IEEE, Los Alamitos, CA., 1988, 81-96.

[ZANI83] ZANIOLO, C. The database language GEM. In *Proceedings of the 1983 ACM SIGMOD Conference* (San Jose, CA., 1983). ACM, New York, 1983, 207-218.

[ZLOO78] ZLOOF, M. Security and Integrity within the Query-By-Example Data Base Management Language. *IBM Research Report RC6982* (February 1978).

Index